Interpreting the Civil War at Museums and Historic Sites

INTERPRETING HISTORY

About the Series

The American Association for State and Local History publishes the *Interpreting History* series in order to provide expert, in-depth guidance in interpretation for history professionals at museums and historic sites. The books are intended to help practitioners expand their interpretation to be more inclusive of the range of American history.

Books in this series help readers:
- quickly learn about the questions surrounding a specific topic,
- introduce them to the challenges of interpreting this part of history, and
- highlight best practice examples of how interpretation has been done by different organizations.

They enable institutions to place their interpretive efforts into a larger context, despite each having a specific and often localized mission. These books serve as quick references to practical considerations, further research, and historical information.

Titles in the Series

Interpreting the Civil War at Museums and Historic Sites

Edited by Kevin M. Levin

ROWMAN & LITTLEFIELD
Lanham • Boulder • New York • London

Published by Rowman & Littlefield
A wholly owned subsidiary of The Rowman & Littlefield Publishing Group, Inc.
4501 Forbes Boulevard, Suite 200, Lanham, Maryland 20706
www.rowman.com

Unit A, Whitacre Mews, 26-34 Stannary Street, London SE11 4AB

British Library Cataloguing in Publication Information Available

Library of Congress Cataloging-in-Publication Data

Names: Levin, Kevin M., 1969–
Title: Interpreting the Civil War at museums and historic sites / Kevin M. Levin.
Description: Lanham : Rowman & Littlefield, 2017. | Series: Interpreting history ; no. 14 |
    Includes bibliographical references and index.
Identifiers: LCCN 2017024842 (print) | LCCN 2017027491 (ebook) | ISBN 9781442273702
    (Electronic) | ISBN 9781442273689 (cloth : alk. paper) | ISBN 9781442273696 (pbk. : alk.
    paper)
Subjects: LCSH: United States—History—Civil War, 1861–1865—Museums. | United
    States—History—Civil War, 1861–1865—Centennial celebrations, etc. | United States—
    History—Civil War, 1861–1865—Historiography. | United States—History—Civil War,
    1861–1865—Battlefields. | Public history—United States. | Collective memory—United
    States.
Classification: LCC E646 (ebook) | LCC E646 .L48 2017 (print) | DDC 973.7—dc23
LC record available at https://lccn.loc.gov/2017024842

Printed in the United States of America

For John Hennessy

Contents

Acknowledgments

First and foremost, I want to thank all of the contributors for agreeing to participate in this project. Their commitments as working public historians and educators would have been justification enough to resist taking on an additional responsibility. The contributors made my job very easy. Their timely responses to multiple drafts and their willingness to probe deeper to highlight lessons for the field will undoubtedly pay off in the form of future programming, new exhibits, and the forging of community relations. The genesis for this project can be traced back to a conversation I had with Bob Beatty at the annual meeting of the American Association for State and Local History in Louisville, Kentucky, in 2015. Following a panel discussion on the ongoing public debate about Confederate monuments, I suggested that a volume in the *Interpreting History* series on the Civil War was needed and that I might be interested in editing it. Thankfully, Bob had already been thinking along the same lines. I greatly appreciate Bob's support and encouragement throughout the process. Bob suggested potential authors, assisted with sketching out some of the topics that needed to be addressed, and helped with reviewing essay drafts. At Rowman & Littlefield I want to thank Charles Harmon, who guided me through the process and helped to keep the project on schedule.

This book is dedicated to my good friend, John Hennessy, who is currently the Chief Historian/Chief of Interpretation at the Fredericksburg & Spotsylvania National Military Park. John is one of those rare triple threats among public historians in the National Park Service. He is a master storyteller, who has never shied away from engaging his audiences around the most controversial topics related to Civil War history. Throughout the Civil War sesquicentennial John was relentless in pushing the park service to think anew about traditional topics of military history and to explore uncharted territory related to race, slavery, and the home front in both new exhibits and programming. Finally, John's scholarship over the years has added immensely to our understanding of Civil War history and has helped to bridge the divide between scholars and general readers. I can think of no one who more fully embodies the virtues of what it means to be a public historian.

Preface

From Centennial to Sesquicentennial

On a blistering hot day, July 21, 1961, an estimated hundred thousand visitors and ten thousand reenactors gathered on the Manassas battlefield in northern Virginia to mark the centennial anniversary of the first major Confederate victory during the Civil War. The reenactment was one of the first commemorative events of the centennial and it was fraught with controversy. The Civil War centennial (1961-1965) was intended to avoid controversy by linking the country's Civil War past with the present around a set of shared values at the height of the Cold War with the Soviet Union.[1] The Virginia Civil War Centennial, Inc. encouraged event organizers "to inspire" their audiences "to be as dedicated to great ideals in a time of peace as our forebears were in a time of war."[2] Americans were encouraged to acknowledge and celebrate their nation's unique place as the defender of freedom and democracy on the world stage. But even as crowds waved Confederate flags and shouted the "rebel yell" following the defeat of Union troops it was clear to some observers that this consensus narrative of the Civil War would be difficult, if not impossible, to sustain.

Centennial event organizers across the nation at historic sites and museums offered visitors a narrative of the Civil War that had changed very little since the end of the war in 1865. The Lost Cause narrative, which took hold in the wake of Confederate defeat, celebrated the Confederacy's brave soldiers and generals such as Robert E. Lee and Thomas "Stonewall" Jackson, who it was believed embodied the highest American virtues. As for slavery, Lost Cause writers argued that it had little or nothing to do with the coming of the war or its outcome. Indeed, these southern writers insisted that race relations were peaceful before the war and that free and enslaved blacks overwhelmingly supported the Confederate war effort. Eventually, the pull of sectional reconciliation and reunion, which was never fully embraced by the veterans themselves, opened the way for Americans North and South to acknowledge the bravery of the men who fought on both sides without having to face the tough questions related to race, slavery, and emancipation. Minimizing or ignoring entirely these issues made it possible for white Americans to celebrate the service and sacrifice of the brave men, who donned the blue and the gray, as the nation was poised to become a world power at the beginning of the twentieth century.

For the large—overwhelmingly white—crowds that attended the centennial's earliest events at battlefields and other historic sites these divisive subjects were overshadowed by the continued influence of the Lost Cause. Problems, however, festered just below the surface. As much as white Americans wanted to celebrate and remember a war that pitted brave soldiers against one another, the continued problem of race served as a reminder that not all was well. Indeed, the images of Lee and Jackson were being challenged on a daily basis by the names of Martin Luther King Jr., Rosa Parks, Medgar Evers, and Emmett Till as well as by the news of school desegregation, lunch counter sit-ins, and Freedom Riders. The civil rights movement presented a challenge to centennial event organizers and participants by casting a shadow on the nation's self-proclaimed status as the leader of the free world.

African Americans such as the civil rights and labor leader A. Philip Randolph cast a critical eye at the overall theme of the centennial: "There is no doubt that this whole Civil War Centennial commemoration is a stupendous brain-washing exercise to make Civil War leaders of the South on par with the Civil War leaders of the North, and to strike a blow against men of color and human dignity."[3] Randolph and other black critics took note of the lack of any reference at most museums and historic sites to the role that African American leaders such as Frederick Douglass and roughly 200,000 black Union soldiers played in ending slavery and in saving the Union. Local newspapers, including the *Richmond Afro-American*, and popular magazines such as *Jet* and *Ebony* offered a powerful counternarrative challenging the central tenets of white America's understanding of the Civil War. Centennial events continued into 1965, but the crowds were smaller and their enthusiasm diminished in response to events on the civil rights front and foreign issues. Confederate flags had been unfurled, but they now stood atop state capital buildings, not simply as a symbol of "Massive Resistance" but also as a defense of a past that had come under increasing attack.[4] While most civil rights activists between 1961 and 1965 concentrated on the more immediate goal of political empowerment rather than on challenging popular perceptions of the Civil War, their actions, along with other factors, would lead to significant changes to how the war and its legacy would be interpreted at museums and historical sites in the decades to follow.

The civil rights movement itself underscored the "unfinished work" of interpretation that was needed at historical institutions. As late as the early 1970s, no major museum had yet to move beyond the Lost Cause narrative to tackle the tough questions related to the history of slavery and its connection to the Civil War and Reconstruction. Reinterpretation came about slowly as a result of ideological resistance within institutions, the availability of artifacts necessary to interpret a more complex past, and the funds necessary to promote research and new exhibits. Museums and other historic sites, however, faced mounting criticism by the end of the 1970s owing to the popularity of Alex Haley's *Roots: The Saga of an American Family* in 1976 and the airing of the twelve-hour television adaptation the following year. The popularity of both pointed to significant gaps in the history being interpreted at historic sites. During this same time advances in the scholarship of slavery as well as of the military history of the war aided the efforts of institutions, which chose to answer calls to expand and revise their interpretations. Historians of slavery continued to uncover the myriad ways in which the actions of slaves—on the plantation, in contraband camps, and eventually in the army itself—contributed to Union victory while military historians broadened their understanding of battles and campaigns to include the experiences of noncombatants and the war's impact on the home front. Such scholarship opened up opportunities for public historians to challenge many deeply engrained institutional narratives with new exhibits and programming.[5]

This new generation of public historians and museum specialists, trained in social history (or "history from the bottom-up"), worked to uncover new stories that gradually moved their institutions away from outdated interpretations. By 1979 the first black reenactors, who performed roles as slaves and free blacks, could be found at Colonial Williamsburg and later at a reconstructed slave quarters at nearby Carter's Grove. In 1994 Colonial Williamsburg staged a mock slave auction that for many visitors exposed the dark side of history for the first time.[6]

Changes could be seen even at the venerable Museum of the Confederacy in Richmond, Virginia, which from its beginning had served more as a shrine to the "Old South" than anything approaching a serious museum. However, by the 1980s, major exhibits, supported in part by the National Endowment for the Humanities and developed on firm academic ground, pushed the MOC further away from its original mission. The debut of "Before Freedom Came" in 1991 earned the MOC national acclaim owing to its comprehensive examination of slavery complete with leg irons and a photograph of a slave whose back starkly revealed the damage caused by his master's whip. Most importantly, the exhibit reinforced that slavery was central to secession, the organization of the Confederate government, and the eventual outcome of the war. Additional exhibits focusing on the Confederate home front and the role of women brought the museum more in line with other institutions, which were now finding ways to address the tough questions of race and slavery in their exhibits and other public programs.

Similar revisions took place at the Stonewall Jackson House in Lexington, Virginia, which, not unlike the MOC, was founded by white women as a shrine to the fallen Confederate. The site enjoyed a steady stream of Civil War enthusiasts through the 1980s, but the museum staff chose to expand their interpretation to situate Jackson as representative of mid-nineteenth-century, white, middle-class culture. Visitors were also exposed to Jackson as an educator, father, and husband and to his religious beliefs as well as his role as slaveholder and the place of the enslaved within his family.

No institution proved to be more important in integrating new scholarship into their exhibits and programming than the National Park Service. Individual parks such as Petersburg National Battlefield began to institute changes by the early 1980s. The gradual shift in how the NPS approached interpretation represented a dramatic break from decades of interpreting Civil War sites as "quiet places of reflection and reconciliation, where veterans gathered to heal rather than cause wounds, where the nation looked for regeneration." By 2000 the NPS introduced a service-wide interpretive plan, called *Holding the High Ground*, which later would serve as a foundation for its sesquicentennial planning. The plan sought to "have parks challenge people with ideas, challenge them to not just understand the nature and horrid expanse of the bloodshed, but the reasons for it, and the consequences of its aftermath." The causes and consequences centered squarely on the subjects of slavery, race, and emancipation.[7]

The steps taken by the NPS to expand their site interpretation served as a foundation for new museums devoted to the Civil War such as Pamplin Historical Park just south of Petersburg, Virginia, in 1999 and the African American Memorial and Civil War Museum, which opened in the predominantly black Shaw Neighborhood of Washington, DC, in 2004. Two years later the American Civil War Museum at Historic Tredegar opened in Richmond.[8]

Changes to the racial profile of local government in communities throughout the South helped to push institutions to embrace a narrative that reflected a more diverse local population and reassured minority groups that they not only would be welcomed, but that their stories would be told. As one visitor noted after visiting Gettysburg, "When you're black, the great battlefield holds mixed messages."[9] Attempts to dedicate new monuments and memorials or mark historic sites with new interpretive markers remained controversial and reflect the fact that the Civil War is still very much a contested landscape, especially for those white Americans who view the war through the lens of ancestors who fought in Confederate ranks and who resist any attempt to suggest that their participation had something to do with the preservation of slavery.

While the shift to a broader and more inclusive interpretation of the Civil War has not been without difficulty, by the eve of the sesquicentennial museums and historic sites were gearing up to offer the public a narrative of the Civil War that had little in common with what was witnessed fifty years earlier during the centennial. Public historians brought to bear new scholarship to a complex story that forced visitors to grapple with difficult questions of history and memory as opposed to celebrating a war that kept the focus tight on the battlefield and a war that pitted brother against brother. Not surprisingly, the NPS led the way by framing their commemorative events around the broad theme of "Civil War to Civil Rights," which placed the subjects of slavery and emancipation at the center of a story that continued through the periods of Reconstruction and Jim Crow. Harpers Ferry opened the NPS's sesquicentennial commemoration three years before its official start in 2011 with programs on John Brown's raid. The staff at Antietam stressed the importance of the battle's connection to emancipation; Fort Sumter dealt with secession; on the grounds of Arlington National Cemetery the staff at Robert E. Lee's former home highlighted the lives of the family's slaves; in Richmond the private and public lives of women were explored[10]; and in Fredericksburg visitors learned about the roughly 10,000 slaves who crossed the Rappahannock River to freedom behind Union lines. Finally, at the Crater in Petersburg, Virginia programs confronted head on some of the most challenging questions related to the participation of black soldiers in the battle and their massacre at the hands of vengeful Confederate soldiers.[11]

Museums and historic sites large and small took advantage of increased interest among the public. Sites located in close proximity to important cultural and historical resources such as battlefields enjoyed the most exposure, but the sesquicentennial rallied staffs in local communities with limited budgets and resources as well as in places not traditionally associated with the Civil War. Museums and historic sites along the Mississippi River interpreted battles that have long been overshadowed by the major fighting in the east at places like Gettysburg, Antietam, and Manassas. Other sites tackled the violent guerrilla fighting that took place in Missouri and Kansas and that divided families and communities throughout the war. Further west historic sites reminded visitors of the steps taken by the US Army to subdue Native Americans during the war. The war's impact on the civilian population, especially in those areas impacted directly by contending armies, introduced audiences to voices that had long been overlooked or filtered through a Lost Cause perspective.

The four years of the sesquicentennial did not take place in isolation from domestic and foreign events. Museums and historic sites responded to a country at war in the Middle East and against terrorism with programs that explored the challenges faced by returning veterans to re-enter society and in dealing with both physical and psychological wounds. The election of the nation's first African American president, increased reports of incidents involving the police and black youth, and the rise of the "Black Lives Matter" movement reinforced for many institutions the importance of leveraging history to inform the present. Arguably, no event did more to focus Americans on the Civil War and its complex legacy than the horrific murder of nine churchgoers committed by Dylann Roof at the Emmanuel African Methodist Episcopal Church in Charleston, South Carolina, on June 17, 2015. The publication of photographs of Roof posing with Confederate battle flags led to its removal from the State House grounds in Columbia. Communities throughout the South and beyond continue to debate the display of Confederate iconography, including monuments and flags, on public grounds.[12]

Organization of the Book

The recently concluded 150th anniversary of the Civil War or Civil War sesquicentennial (2011-2015) is an ideal place to assess these changes at our nation's historic sites and museums. The essays that follow take a broad look at how museums and historic sites engaged audiences throughout the sesquicentennial. They represent institutions that continue to face unique challenges depending on their location, size, audience, and access to cultural and historical resources. Authors assess different levels of planning at their respective institutions from the development and implementation of broad themes to specific programs, including their strengths and weaknesses. In addition to looking back, many of the essays that follow offer concrete advice for public historians and institutions as they move forward from a period of piqued interest among the public in the war.

Virginia proved to be a popular destination during the sesquicentennial. The state includes some of the most popular Civil War battlefields, from Manassas just outside of Washington, DC, to the ring of sites around Petersburg and up and down the Shenandoah Valley. The former Confederate capital of Richmond is a city with tremendous historical and cultural assets and steeped in monuments, statuary, roads, schools, and other public spaces that honor the memory of the Confederacy and its iconic figures. Until recently this increasingly diverse city all but erased from its landscape the fact it was also the second largest slave-trading city in the country during the Antebellum Period. It is the city where Abraham Lincoln stepped off a small boat and walked through its streets after it fell to Union forces (which included United States Colored Troops) in April 1865. In chapter 1, "Among the Ruins: Creating and Interpreting the American Civil War in Richmond," Christy S. Coleman examines the history of the Museum of the Confederacy (1896) and American Civil War Center at Historic Tredegar (2006) before their recent merger as the American Civil War Center, in which she currently serves as co-president. Coleman highlights the many challenges of interpreting the Civil War in a racially diverse city and one where passions can be easily excited. According to Coleman, "Museums can and should be powerful advocates for narrative change by engaging and challenging their communities to consider new research and the questions raised by it."

Moving north from Richmond Mark Benbow explores the challenges of interpreting Union occupation in Arlington County, Virginia. Many visitors associate Virginia with the Confederacy, but the area around the Washington, DC, remained in Union hands for much of the war and many of its residents were loyal to the United States. In chapter 2, "Billy Yank, Not Johnny Reb: Focusing Civil War Exhibits on the Union in Virginia," Benbow demonstrates how a museum with limited resources can complicate the narrative of the war in Virginia by challenging the assumption that the "South = Confederacy" and encouraging visitors to reconsider "the complicated realities of regional loyalties." The essay also explores recent efforts to interpret Reconstruction and the challenges of reaching out to the community's African American population.

The Civil War will always be associated with the great battlefields in places like Maryland, Pennsylvania, Virginia, and Georgia. For Daniel Joyce, Douglas Dammann, and Jennifer Edginton this reality raises a number of unique challenges for their museum devoted to the Civil War in Kenosha, Wisconsin. In chapter 3, "A Civil War Museum in Kenosha, Wisconsin?" the authors outline the development of the museum's overall narrative, which focuses on the connection between the home front and the military and the larger story of how the war impacted the Upper Midwest. Their use of traditional exhibitions and new technologies to enhance the visitor experience of life in camp, the battlefield, and the veterans' experience ought to serve as a model for museums operating far from the central events of the war.

In chapter 4, "Civil War Public History For the Next Generation," veteran teacher James Percoco shares his experience working with local museums and historic sites to establish internships for his students. Located in northern Virginia, Percoco worked with a wide range of institutions, including the National Park Service. Among other things, students took part in projects to commemorate important events, assumed roles as first-person interpreters, worked as guides, and catalogued artifacts. Working on site enhanced students' classroom experience in numerous ways. A number of Percoco's students have gone on to careers as public historians. A successful collaboration with museums and historic sites will go far to ensuring the development of the next generation of public historians.

As noted above, even before the official start of the sesquicentennial the National Park Service worked to connect individual sites connected to the Civil War and beyond around the narrative: "From Civil War to Civil Rights." Park Rangers and front line interpreters were encouraged to interpret and connect their sites to broader themes related to the causes and consequences of the war and their implications for the history of race and slavery through the 1960s. The broader focus was intended to move park staff away from narrow site interpretation of battle and campaigns to the discussion of larger issues that connect the past with the present. John Rudy, who trains Park Rangers as part of the NPS's Interpretive Development Program, assesses the efforts, in chapter 5, to expand interpretation and suggests that while the NPS has much to celebrate, more work needs to be done to transform parks into "sites of social conscience and civic engagement."

Between 2010 and 2014, the Georgia Historical Society launched and implemented the Civil War 150 Historical Marker Project. Coupling an older (and some say outmoded) form of public history—historical markers—with modern scholarship and the latest technology, the project was designed to promote tourism while presenting a broader, more inclusive picture of the war. Over a five-year period, GHS installed twenty new markers that told stories about people and events previously overlooked in public spaces of Georgia dedicated to Civil War history. In chapter 6, "New Wine in Old Bottles: Using Historical Markers to Reshape Public Memory of the Civil War," W. Todd Groce shows how a traditional public history tool can be used to bridge the gap between academic historians and the general public and bring modern scholarship to a wider audience. Among other things, Groce explores how older markers were revised and new subjects selected, how the program worked as a form of public outreach and, more importantly, how it empowered segments of local communities whose stories had been overlooked.

W. Eric Emerson, from the South Carolina Department of Archives and History, is on the front lines of the debate about how to display the Confederate Flag that was recently removed from the State House grounds in Columbia shortly after the deadly shooting in Charleston. Plans call for the flag to be displayed as part of the permanent Civil War exhibit at the South Carolina Relic Room. In chapter 7, "Commemoration, Conflict, and Constraints: The Saga of the Confederate Flag at the South Carolina State House," Emerson outlines the history of the Confederate battle flag at the State House as well as the challenges of how to interpret an artifact that is at the center of our current discussion about the history and memory of the Confederacy. Emerson offers concrete suggestions on how to properly interpret the flag in a museum setting, which should be particularly helpful to public historians working on exhibits that feature potentially polarizing artifacts and interpretations.

The ongoing debate about the display of the Confederate flag, monuments, and other forms of iconography is likely to have a profound impact on the work of public historians for the foreseeable future. Public historians and educators tend to approach this subject narrowly by interpreting monuments as sites of memory and commemoration. Such an approach offers important insights into how communities have chosen what to remember and celebrate from the past and what events and individuals were forgotten or minimized. While these discussions are important they have the potential to ignore or give short shrift to issues of justice and racial discrimination in communities struggling to come to terms with their public commemorative sites. In chapter 8, "Getting to the Heart: The Intersections of Confederate Iconography, Race Relations, and Public History in America," Dina Bailey and Nicole Moore explore how public historians can engage communities in these sensitive but important discussions.

Public historians working at museums and historic sites focused on the Civil War era are tasked with interpreting a period of history that remains controversial. Many visitors are deeply invested in historic sites such as battlefields and artifacts as well as harbor strong convictions about the cause of the war, its consequences, and the importance of slavery. As

Christy Coleman suggests in the opening chapter, interpreting the Civil War is "not for the weak of heart." But if the essays that comprise this book demonstrate anything, it is that public historians can successfully navigate these potential landmines by embracing sound scholarship in shaping exhibits and programs and by listening closely to and establishing working relationships with different constituencies within their communities. While the size of crowds has certainly diminished since the close of the sesquicentennial, the ongoing controversy surrounding the display of the Confederate battle flag and monuments in communities throughout the country will likely keep the memory of the war front and center for many Americans. Public historians can play a vital role in engaging Americans about this important period in history as well as questions related to how it continues to shape our communities and our hopes for the future.

Notes

1. Joan M. Zenzen, *Battling For Manassas: The Fifty-Year Preservation Struggle at Manassas National Battlefield Park* (University Park: The Pennsylvania State University Park, 1998), 68-71; on the centennial, see Robert J. Cook, *Troubled Commemoration: The American Civil War Centenial, 1961–1965* (Baton Rouge: Louisiana State University Press, 2007).
2. Quoted in Kevin M. Levin, *Remembering the Battle of the Crater: War as Murder* (Lexington: University Press of Kentucky, 2012), 114.
3. Quoted in Levin, *Remembering the Battle of the Crater*, 116.
4. On the history of the Confederate battle flag, see John M. Coski, *The Confederate Battle Flag: America's Most Embattled Emblem* (Cambridge: Harvard University Press, 2005).
5. W. Fitzhugh Brundage, *The Southern Past: A Clash of Race and Memory* (Cambridge: Harvard University Press, 2005), 293–303.
6. Anders Greenspan, *Creating Colonial Williamsburg* (Washington, DC: Smithsonian Institution Press, 2002), 148–72.
7. The scholarly foundation for this initiative is explored in Robert K. Sutton ed., *Rally on the High Ground: The National Park Service Symposium on the Civil War* (Washington, DC: Eastern National, 2001); Dwight T. Pitcaithley, "'A Cosmic Threat': The National Park Service Addresses the Causes of the American Civil War," in *Slavery and Public History: The Tough Stuff of American Memory*, eds. James O. Horton and Louis E. Horton (New York: The New Press, 2006), 169–86.
8. James J. Broomall, "The Interpretation Is A-Changin': Memory, Museums and Public History in Central Virginia," *The Journal of the Civil War Era* 3:1(March 2013): 114–25.
9. Quoted in Levin, *Remembering the Battle of the Crater*, 131; on the continued challenge to attract African Americans and other minorities to Civil War sites, see Ta Nehisi-Coates, "Why Do So Few Blacks Study the Civil War?" *The Atlantic*, The Civil War Issue, https://www.theatlantic.com/magazine/archive/2012/02/why-do-so-few-blacks-study-the-civil-war/308831/.
10. Ashley Whitehead Luskey and Robert M. Dunkerly, "From Women's History to Gender History: Revamping Interpretive Programming at Richmond National Battlefield Park," *Civil War History* 62:2 (June 2016): 149–69.

11. John Hennessy, "Touchstone: The Sesquicentennial, the National Park Service, and a Changing Nation," *Common-Place* 14, no. 2 (2014) url: http://www.common-place-archives.org/vol-14/no-02/hennessy/#.WLsfGRxAvFw; Emmanuel Dabney, Beth Parnicza, and Kevin M. Levin, "Interpreting Race, Slavery, and United States Colored Troops at Civil War Battlefields," *Civil War History* 62:2 (June 2016): 131–48.
12. Modupe Labode, "Reconsideration of Memorials and Monuments," *History News: The Magazine of the American Association for State and Local History* 71:4 (2016): 7–11.

CHAPTER 1

Among the Ruins

Creating and Interpreting the American Civil War in Richmond

Christy S. Coleman

TOURISTS AND MUSEUMGOERS EXPLORE the American Civil War by visiting thousands of monuments, museums, and historical markers scattered across the United States that document its battles and events. Collectively, these places should remind us that the Civil War altered everything in America—the landscape, economy, politics, social structure and more. However, exactly what view of the War's cause, course, and legacy were and are visitors getting from these experiences? A recent study by the Pew Research Center found that more than 48 percent of respondents believe the primary cause of the Civil War was state's rights (tariffs, nullification debates, etc.) compared to the 38 percent noting slavery as its root cause.[1] Those in public history and academia recognize the causes for the war are deeply intertwined. Yet translating a more nuanced interpretation to the general populace proves challenging for many reasons.

The transformation to a more comprehensive national narrative that explores the multiplicity of issues and perspectives has been painfully slow. Museums reveled in being able to showcase collections of "war relics," without engaging visitors about the reasons Americans went to war with one another. Popular culture played a significant and often damaging role throughout the twentieth century with how the War was remembered. From D. W. Griffith's *Birth of A Nation* and MGM's *Gone With The Wind* to more recent *Gods and Generals*, *Cold Mountain*, and the television miniseries the *North and South*, a romanticism engulfed the deadliest period of our shared past. Complicating matters further, monuments memorializing those who fought on both sides make it far more difficult to glean lessons from this past. What we end up with are stories of honorable men who either fought to save their homes or fought for the freedom of millions of enslaved people. Neither is fully accurate but these monuments are the most enduring challenge to a more comprehensive public narrative.

This is far from surprising when one considers most Civil War sites and battlefields are principally in the South. Subsequently, how the American Civil War is remembered and interpreted has been skewed by those often sympathetic to the Confederacy. The most prominent museums or sites interpreting the War throughout most of the twentieth century were the Museum of the Confederacy and the National Park Service. For decades, NPS avoided controversy by simply focusing on military actions and leaders. It was not until the late 1990s that political and social issues became a consistent part of NPS battlefield interpretation of the War. But there was another initiative afoot in Richmond, Virginia, that proved equally powerful in helping to stem the tide toward a more inclusive and complete public narrative. This is important because as the former Capital of the Confederacy, how the Civil War was interpreted in Richmond had and has a rippling effect. Two organizations were at the fore of this important change: the Museum of the Confederacy and the upstart American Civil War Center at Historic Tredegar.

How Shall We Remember?

From the earliest days of the Confederacy, the importance of building a sense of nationhood was deemed paramount. With *"each State acting in its sovereign and independent character,"* the Confederate States of America held together a fragile alliance.[2] But it shared three key ideas: state sovereignty, white supremacy, and slavery as the natural condition for persons of African descent. However when the Confederacy lost the War, the narrative shifted. Slavery disappeared as a cause as rapidly as Richmond's burned commercial district where human beings were trafficked. Shockoe Bottom, the second most lucrative slave market in the country, was scorched to ruins by the Confederates. Soon, the underlying cause for secession by every single Confederate state was all but erased despite volumes of documents making clear each state's intent for withdrawing from the Union.

Over the course of several decades, Richmond and other communities across the country were able to frame the War and its meaning from personal perspectives and social motives. Everyone could define their heroes and villains without interference—or, quite frankly, without deeper critical or historical analyses. By doing so, it was far easier to focus on key political or military figures placing them in a "good versus bad" vernacular. When slavery was removed or defined as less significant in the conflict, other more palatable re- membrances could take root unencumbered. As a result, the public narrative was woefully incomplete but deeply held across generations. Whether derived from familial connection, ideological affiliation, or simply because one likes a story about "an underdog," the American Civil War remains a revered period. Is there little wonder it is among the most written about yet most contentious topics in American history?

The earliest Civil War monuments and markers were placed in the immediate aftermath of the War to honor and rebury the dead. The federal government oversaw reburial of its 300,000 plus dead in 73 national cemeteries established for that purpose. The largest was established at Arlington, the plantation home of Robert E. Lee. It was intended to be a permanent reminder of the carnage wrought upon the nation. Since the Confederate States of America had no system for adequate burial of its dead, bodies were often left in shallow graves on the field where men fell in battle. Outraged by what they perceived as the Union's disregard for their dead, memorial societies led by middle to upper class white women organized to rectify the situation. Throughout the South, the soldiers' aid societies oversaw the gruesome task of locating and transporting tens of thousands of soldiers' bodies from numerous battlefields. They also established cemeteries for their Confederate dead or designated areas within existing burial grounds like Hollywood Cemetery. They initially built modest monuments to serve as reminders of the sacrifices of their dead like their counterparts in the North, but the scale would grow considerably during the next boom of monument building.

In 1866, Richmond's Soldiers' Aid Society became the Ladies Hollywood Memorial Association (LHMA) with the sole intent to ensure their loved and revered ones would not be forgotten. In 1869, they erected a ninety-foot tall pyramid in Hollywood Cemetery to be a beacon and reminder to future generations. "Let our children grow up, to foster it—making this sacred Spot, more and more attractive, each succeeding year, worthy of being the deposit of our heart's love, honour and gratitude!"[3] Their work was duplicated in many communities throughout the South resulting in more monuments, markers, and memorials. But few compared to those eventually constructed in Richmond.

Shortly after the death of Robert E. Lee in 1870, many in Richmond and throughout the South wanted to honor him in grand fashion. The LHMA partnered with the Lee Memorial Association, a group of former Confederate officers. During a joint meeting to discuss the matter, their first order of business was to find a suitable location to build a monument to their hero. Colonel C. S. Venable argued successfully and eloquently for Richmond to be the choice.

> . . . we say, here in Richmond, which was founded by the companions of his knightly ancestors; at Richmond, the objective point of those attacks made with all the accumulated resources of modern warfare, which he repelled for four long years; Richmond, where lie many of the brave soldiers who went gaily to death at his bidding; some, who fell with their last looks upon the spires of her temples; others nursed in their dying hours by the tender hands of her women; and others still who gave their souls to God and their bodies to the enemy at Gettysburg, brought hither by the loving care of the same devoted women.[4]

With a new grand boulevard planned in the western outskirt of downtown, Richmond was the ideal location. Unveiled to an estimated 100,000 people in May 1890, the Lee Monument was among the grandest built in the United States at the time. The success of that endeavor led to four more added to Monument Avenue over the next three decades: J. E. B. Stuart (1907), Jefferson Davis (1907), Thomas J. "Stonewall" Jackson (1919), and

Matthew Fountain Maury (1929). Embedded in granite, the accomplishments of each could be read about by visitors while simultaneously speaking to honor and sacrifice. The placement of the Robert E. Lee statue in 1890 quickly made Richmond a must-see destination for the Confederate-memory faithful and those curious from around the world.

The death of Jefferson Davis in 1889 provided the opportunity for the LHMA to present more expansive ideas to a broad audience of people from throughout the South. Led by Isobel Stewart Bryan and others, they created a new entity called the Confederate Memorial Literary Society, dedicated to saving the Brockenbrough home that served as the Executive Mansion for the Davis family during the War. The women sent notices throughout the South collecting the "relics" of the Confederate generation. They established a network of Regents—one prominent woman representing each of the Confederate states—and Vice Regents—women from Richmond to coordinate each state's display. Virginia's first Regent was Robert E. Lee's daughter, who ensured some of the first artifacts in the collection were his wartime possessions. The provenance on the collection was astounding, with direct ties and stories that accompanied each artifact.

With feverish intensity, the CMLS raised money, collected artifacts, and completely refurbished the mansion. Named the Confederate Museum, it opened in 1896 to grand fanfare and visitors from throughout the country and around the world. The Confederate Museum became a beacon to generations of white Southerners intent on preserving the memory and legacy of their ancestors. Thousands of other items followed, almost all donated by the original users or their families. By 1905, more than half the collection was in place. Few organizations or museums could rival the items amassed. Recognized as the leading organization for Confederate memorabilia, the US War Department transferred 327 flags between 1905 and 1906 captured during the War. With the success of the museum, it could be easily argued the Lost Cause flourished in Richmond unfettered for almost eighty years.

But societal upheaval against the status quo during the 1950s and 1960s impacted cultural institutions. Increased intensity of the modern civil rights movement challenged the mythology of "the Old South," aided by new scholarship from social historians. Segregationists entrenched using rhetoric of the Lost Cause and many symbols, particularly the Army of Northern Virginia battle flag, to advance their concerns. The "Confederate" flag was used as a symbol of resistance to integration and equal rights. For African Americans that flag had long been associated with violence inflicted upon them and their allies. In addition, jurisdictions throughout the south, Richmond included, renamed schools, bridges, highways, and other public spaces after Confederate icons in protest. Ironically, a plethora of Civil War centennial observances were taking place all over the country—but particularly in the South. Even though it benefited from the attention and focus of the centennial, the Confederate Museum was thrust into modernity as criticisms mounted about its antiquated facilities and stories. The Regents began serious discussions about how best to proceed.

When Change Comes

By 1970, the Confederate Museum was facing significant financial difficulties. Shifting political and social attitudes along with early encroachment of the Medical College of Virginia (later VCU Health Systems) led to significant visitation declines. The decision was made to alter the CMLS's focus from being a shrine "for" the Confederacy to a museum "about" the Confederacy. As a result, several transformations took place. The Brockenbrough House was among the first placed on the National Register of Historic Places. A robust, multi-year fundraising campaign was undertaken to protect and restore what became known as the White House of the Confederacy to its 1860s appearance. Additionally, a modern museum facility to house the remarkable collection of artifacts and manuscripts was desperately needed. The House Regent was replaced by a trained museum professional. The Regents restructured, eventually forming a modern board of directors. The museum's name was also changed to the Museum of the Confederacy (MOC). The doors of its new museum opened to the public in 1976, coinciding with the American Bicentennial celebrations.

In its September 27, 1976, cover story on "The South Today," *TIME* magazine hailed the changes at the museum. Its renowned collection became far more accessible to scholars around the country who mined its vast resources. Visitation rebounded with guests coming from around the world. A wave of new scholarship based on its archival materials confronted Lost Cause memorialization delving deeper into the Antebellum and War periods. Few subjects were off limits including the actions, attitudes, and private lives of Confederate icons. Meanwhile, the team of professional museum staff continued to transform the organization envisioning new opportunities due to a variety of factors, most notably the changing demographic within Richmond's populace and governance.

"Victory in Defeat," an exhibition unveiled in 1985, took the first critical look at the Lost Cause narrative and its impact in museums. It was a resounding success. With a major grant from the National Endowment for the Humanities, the museum completed restoration of the White House of the Confederacy with much of the original furniture and accoutrements, reopening in 1988. Perhaps the most groundbreaking exhibition developed by the museum was 1991's "Before Freedom Came." It was considered one of the most important exhibitions ever attempted on slavery, and another element was critical to its success. Active engagement with Richmond's African American community around the exhibition's themes and imagery resulted in long-overdue conversations about the meaning of the Confederacy to them. The museum's exhibits and lectures broke new ground by tackling subjects previously ignored or suppressed, to critical acclaim. But it also drew disdain from many who hated the shift away from honoring Confederate heroes. Some of the disgruntled included the museum's key contributors and its board of trustees. In response, some resigned while others retrenched.

But the 1990s brought a different transformation at the organization. Run exclusively by white women since 1890, the museum added its first men and its first African American to the board of trustees. Meanwhile, the museum's staff continued to roll out exceptional exhibitions about the War that few organizations matched in terms of intellectual scope and artifact abundance. In 1993, "Embattled Emblem" examined the Confederate battle flag and its legacy, from both the 1860s and the civil rights era. "A Woman's War" examined the important role women of various economic and social stations played during the War. It went far beyond the idea of "keep the home fires burning" to women seizing political power within the bounds allowed to those taking on non-traditional roles. But an additional threat loomed for the museum.

While the museum has transformed itself from shrine to education institution, public perception remained a challenge in an increasingly diverse population. By the late 1990s, the very name—Museum of the Confederacy—impacted visitation and funding options. These realities severely threatened the museum's ability to continue to properly care for what is arguably the largest and finest collection of Confederate and Civil War–related artifacts, archives, and manuscripts in the world. Making matters worse, access to the museum and White House were severely compromised as the Virginia Commonwealth University Health System started a massive building expansion of high-rise medical buildings around the museum footprint. Visitors were forced to negotiate a complicated streetscape with inadequate parking and access to reach the White House and museum.

Seeking outside strategic assistance, the museum called upon colleagues at the American Association of Museums. Among numerous suggestions for improvement was the recommendation that the museum change its name to become more welcoming and accessible to a growing and diverse population. The recommendation was not well received. Despite all the stellar work done for almost two decades, the backlash was swift within the organization's board. The museum director was terminated and several members of the board left in solidarity believing the majority's actions doomed the organization to collapse. Among the first things done by a new director was place a "Confederate flag" outside the entrance to the Museum of the Confederacy, crippling relationships built with Richmond's increasingly diverse community.

Among those resigning was MOC's board chair. Alex Wise was convinced a broader narrative about the War was required to build healthy communities and our nation. He was also convinced the conversation had to happen in Richmond. Honing his ideas, he began sharing the vision around Richmond and the country. He garnered support and assistance from the nation's leading scholars of Civil War history. He sought out private collectors and other museum colleagues to learn best practices. He met with leading philanthropists to bring this dream to fruition. Echoing Stephen Weil's work, "Good museums matter, good museums make a difference. . . . The very things that make a museum good are its intent to make a positive difference in the quality of people's lives."[5] Alex and his partners developed a plan for a new kind of Civil War museum.

With philanthropic backing and support from academics, the Tredegar National Civil War Foundation Museum was established in 1999. Founding board members represented all regions of the country and reflected the inclusion and diversity of the nation. The initial plan was for a massive complex to include exhibition galleries where stories could be told about the War's causes, consequences, and legacies from three crucial perspectives—Union, Confederate, and African American. It was an audacious plan that garnered widespread support. In 2000, the Richmond National Battlefield Park (NPS) announced it would relocate its visitor center to the historic Tredegar Iron Works site. NPS brought its new narrative to the visitor center project and rolled political motivations into interpretations at its twelve surrounding battlefields. Both Tredegar projects were going well until the 9/11 terrorist attacks shattered financial markets, crippled tourism, and all but decimated the new museum's funding efforts. Fortunately by 2003, hope returned and the Tredegar National Civil War Foundation Museum was renamed the American Civil War Center at Historic Tredegar (ACWC). Work immediately began on its new museum to be housed in the 1861

Gun Foundry—the very place where half of all Confederate cannon were manufactured. Many viewed efforts at Tredegar as an alternative to perceived outdated narratives and entrenchment at the Museum of the Confederacy.

During this period, many Richmond civic and community leaders decided the landscape had to reflect more of Richmond's diverse history, particularly the accomplishments of African Americans. They desperately wanted to balance the imagery visitors experienced when they came to the city. The first new monument depicting an African American was "Boatman," dedicated in 1993 and placed on Brown's Island as part of the riverfront development program. The statue was designed to honor black men who were crucial to enterprise involving the river. Soon after, a tribute to Henry "Box" Brown was placed at the popular Shockoe Bottom neighborhood. The most stunning addition to the landscape was "Lincoln," dedicated in 2003 at Historic Tredegar. The monument was a gift of the United States Historical Society to the Richmond National Battlefield Park of the National Park Service. Several thousand guests came to the dedication ceremony, but they were greeted by a few Confederate heritage protestors donning battle flags while a plane flew overhead with a banner reading "Sic Temper Tyrannis." Not only is the Latin phrase meaning "Death to Tyrants" Virginia's motto, it was also spoken by Lincoln's assassin, John Wilkes Booth.

Conversely there were several flashpoints in Richmond around Confederate imagery. Monument Avenue's massive monuments were defaced with greater frequency. Many, including Richmond's African American community, raged against an image of Robert E. Lee included in a huge banner installation on the city's floodwall in 2000. The Lee banner was burned by what police described as a Molotov cocktail, and the culprit was never found. When attempts were made to replace it, a city council member railed against it while vulgar threats and racial epithets were hurled at him. The United Daughters of the Confederacy and the Sons of Confederate Veterans lodged their own complaints about what was happening. They strongly believed Lee's image deserved to be among the honored persons depicted. Robert W. Barbour Jr., commander of the Virginia Division of the Sons of Confederate Veterans, called for a swift and thorough investigation of the vandalism, labeling it "nothing [less] than a crime of hatred toward Southerners and Confederate history."[6]

Against this backdrop, the MOC was once again facing a very tumultuous period that included significant loss of income from visitation and donations. The museum had to find a way to reinvent itself, again. In 2005 the board of trustees and its new director began to review its options to remain true to the museum's mission of educating the public about the Confederate era and its legacy while remaining accessible and relevant in the twenty-first century.

Few ideas were off the table. There was even a proposal to move the White House of the Confederacy to the Tredegar Iron Works site. Instead a decision was made to establish a "system" of museum sites. They believed a network of well planned, state-of-the-art museums throughout Virginia would accomplish the museum's strategic goals. Several locations in Virginia were considered, including Fredericksburg, Hampton, and Appomattox. Of these, Appomattox was chosen because of robust Civil War visitation at the nearby NPS site and outstanding community support. The MOC started an ambitious fundraising initiative to bring its vision to fruition.

Richmond was awash in Civil War projects that were pushing envelopes on several fronts. The NPS Visitor Center brought 70,000 visitors downtown adding to the 150,000 at its battlefields. The American Civil War Center at Historic Tredegar opened its doors to the public in October 2006. Scholars, the public, and the media hailed its signature exhibition "In the Cause of Liberty" as a major advance in the interpretation of the War because of its mission to "tell the whole story of the conflict that shapes our lives." Many called it the first museum to tell its story from three perspectives—Union, Confederate, and African American—all under the same roof, in the same gallery, side by side. It was also praised as an ambitious undertaking started in a city known for one dominant narrative. The center brought new and younger audiences to an often-contentious history but also challenged visitors to consider the impact of the War. That element was perhaps what set it apart from others. There was a conscious decision toward relevant and usable history.

When the center's founding director departed eighteen months after the museum's opening, deep concern about whether or not the strides made would be abandoned by a new director. But the board was steadfast in its desire to be innovative. With a new director on board (yours truly), the task presented was how best to be at the forefront of commemoration of the sesquicentennial of the Civil War. The board seemed fixed on facility expansion, but what was needed most was reconnecting with various communities and constituencies in Richmond. Given the organization's size, there was no way it could have the impact desired without strategic partners.

Fortunately others were thinking about the looming anniversary of the War. Several states announced commissions to commemorate its 150th anniversary, including Virginia. The center's director was asked to participate in discussions with the Virginia State Commission for the Civil War sesquicentennial. It was clear from those early meetings that the state wanted a deeper narrative—so much so, much of its stated goals mirrored the center's mission and approach. But Richmond itself was at a standstill about the event despite the fact that half of the War's major battles and three quarters of its casualties occurred between Richmond and Washington. Community funders and corporations were leery about supporting Civil War history initiatives, labeling them too controversial. It seemed a hopeless endeavor despite the fact that the city and regional tourism entities knew there would be a spike in visitation around the event. Early surveys conducted by Richmond Regional Tourism found Civil War enthusiasts wanted to retrace key events in the War. Unlike Gettysburg or even Washington, Richmond stood on the precipice because it was at the center of the conflict all four years of the War.

A number of cultural and academic leaders came together—first informally—to discuss how Richmond could seize the moment. Fortunately there was also a belief that this was an opportunity to enhance the narrative—to reinvent how Richmond shared its Civil War past and other cultural assets. Through strategic partnerships with seventeen other entities representing cultural, educational, and academic institutions, the group unanimously decided that Richmond's sesquicentennial observances would not be called an anniversary or a celebration, but instead a commemoration of the Civil War *and* emancipation.

Work began immediately on several fronts but funding was critical. The center worked closely with Richmond Regional Tourism and NPS to establish a "Gateway to the Civil War" at Historic Tredegar. Centrally located with easy access and ample parking, the Historic Tredegar site was a logical starting point for exploring the Civil War and emancipation in Richmond. After renovating space in the Pattern Building, the new visitor center opened in 2011. Visitation at Historic Tredegar spiked 33 percent, and other locations throughout the city saw significant increases as well.

The following year, the MOC opened its Museum of the Confederacy at Appomattox. The new museum was very well done with strong interpretive themes that delved into the postwar years. But it couldn't evade controversy. Confederate heritage groups protested the opening because the museum's promenade flew the flags of each state that formed the Confederacy, but did not feature the "Confederate Flag." Protestors lined the roadway leading to the museum for days waving battle flags. Some residents in proximity of the museum actually erected large flagpoles to don their Confederate flags. It was another example of the gulf between Confederate heritage groups and the MOC. But the museum continued to press forward. In response, it reinstalled the "Embattled Emblem" exhibition updating content to reflect more recent controversies and events.

Meanwhile the Future of Richmond's Past (FoRP) coalition established to commemorate the War was growing. The larger group worked tirelessly to create citywide events that included the Black History Museum and Cultural Center, the Elegba Folklore Society, the Virginia Historical Society, and many others. FoRP hosted a series of community conversations all over the city to engage residents about unresolved issues around the war and its legacies in the life of the city. In time, more than two thousand people voluntarily joined mailing lists and engaged regularly with the conversations over the five-year period. Their diverse voices informed programming around not only what the community wanted to see, but also what it needed to see. The first Civil War and Emancipation Day Weekend drew more than four thousand residents and visitors despite dreary, wet weather conditions. The response to the venture was overwhelmingly positive. The ethnicity, gender, and age diversity evident among participants that day was astounding. No one could have imagined the initiative would have such a resonant effect.

When We Become Whole

Because of the ongoing work of the FoRP coalition, ACWM and MOC were often at the fore of activities and formed an alliance beyond the commemoration activities. The MOC was gracious in sharing its collections for the center's exhibition. They began hosting prominent scholars together. Then conversations took an interesting turn among key donors and leadership of both organizations. One donor in particular asked the most audacious question of all—what if you merged? The timing was auspicious given the center's completed capital campaign to expand facilities at Historic Tredegar. But consolidating the Museum of the Confederacy and the American Civil War Center was an idea discussed years before the center even opened its doors. It never materialized because each organization's mission was distinct and concerns over member and donor expectations were paramount.

Serious deliberations began in 2012 when the Appomattox project was completed. After highly confidential discussions among members of both institutions' directors, trustees, major donors, and other key constituents, the decision was made in 2013 to move forward with the consolidation. The museums combined world-class collections of Civil War artifacts, with significant historic sites in the War's political and geographic center—Richmond. Meaningful exhibits, lectures, and educational program concepts could be explored in ways changing audiences were hungry to experience.

But leadership was an unresolved issue. Who would lead it? Having served on both boards and deeply respected by Richmond's citizenry for his work at the University of Richmond and Future of Richmond's Past, Edward L. Ayers was selected to serve as the new museum's chair. A new board was formed as each organization selected twelve members to serve the entity. The board also decided that given the massive scope of work to be done prior to opening, it would establish a co-CEO leadership structure during the transitional period.

Marketing and research efforts continued informing how the museum branded its mission. Clean and elegant, ACWM's logo features three outlined Civil War figures—a woman, an African American, and a soldier. The icon evokes the War's impact on all Americans and visually demonstrates ACWM's commitment to tell stories with depth, nuance, and clarity. Under the image, the tagline infuses the words Confederacy, Union, and Freedom to further convey the museum's mission and goals. The overarching goal is to communicate that the AWCM is a place where families, casual visitors, Civil War travelers, school groups, researchers, and the local community will be able to explore new themes, ideas, and experiences that are immersive, intellectually challenging, and emotionally engaging.

There was little doubt where the new museum would be built. Centrally located, the Tredegar site has intrinsic advantages that favor its role as a national museum. Nearby are a number of important Civil War–related sites, including those not often associated with it. They include the Lumpkin's Jail Archaeological Site and Slave Burial Ground. In addition, the Slave Trail along the James River, where tens of thousands of slaves were bought and sold, allows visitors to retrace that experience alone or on powerful tours. Tredegar is also nestled along the river between Confederate burial grounds at Hollywood Cemetery and a multitude of War memorials. The site also provides a fitting vista from which to contemplate the enormity of the passion and furor as guests literally look upon the ruins of bridges where people fled the city as Union troops advanced to claim it in 1865.

After months of careful planning, the creation of the American Civil War Museum (ACWM) was announced in November 2013 to the public. Its mission: *To be the preeminent center for the exploration of the American Civil War and its legacies from multiple perspectives: Union and Confederate, enslaved and free African Americans, soldiers and civilians.* The new institution comprises three locations: the White House of the Confederacy, Historic Tredegar, and the Museum of the Confederacy–Appomattox. The response was overwhelmingly positive, but there were also very angry people who felt that the MOC had put the final death nail in Confederate memory. The MOC's CEO received hundreds of vile letters, emails, and calls, in some cases threatening or wishing bodily harm. There were also those who felt the center had been co-opted by wealthy interests wanting to give legitimacy to the Confederacy all along—even proposing it was a conspiracy from its founding. The ACWM's CEO received letters questioning ethnic loyalties while a KKK-affiliated organization established petitions for ouster. But the museum was prepared for most of this rancor. With the help of a public relations firm, the museum prepared in advance a series of responses to criticism distributing it to every level of the organization and key community stakeholders to ensure

Figure 1.1. American Civil War Museum, new facility in 2018. Courtesy American Civil War Museum

the messages were consistent. Museum leadership also reached out to a variety of supporting and opposing groups offering to speak directly with them rather than allow rumors to take hold. Knowing a considerable portion of existing members, particularly from the MOC, would withdraw financial support, the museum planned for a 40 percent decline in membership and contributions in its first combined budget. The reality was closer to 30 percent, which the museum has not regained to date.

Richmond continued exploring its Civil War past in new, more inclusive ways through the FoRP's Civil War and Emancipation program. The culminating event took place April 2–4, 2015, on the Capital Square Grounds. Each representing organization offered programs, new works, and interpretations. Artists using powerful imagery and simulated flames illuminated areas surrounding the capital where fires destroyed buildings during the fall of Richmond in 1865. Throngs followed the paths of Union troops and that of Abraham Lincoln when he came to survey the city 150 years prior. Over the course of the weekend, more people converged at the capital and other sites than could be adequately counted. Among the event's keynote speakers were the governor of Virginia, the mayor of Richmond, and council members, all who came to lay witness and praise the endeavor. "It was a testament of just how far we've come," said Mayor Dwight C. Jones.[7]

Unfortunately, later that summer the rest of the country was in turmoil. The murder of nine black churchgoers in Charleston by a young white supremacist sparked outrage. Fueling the outcry was an image of the murderer with a gun waving a small Confederate flag. This was the first time the new ACWM would be called upon to provide historical context during a time of national crisis. In several short weeks, the museum fielded dozens of calls conducting interviews with news outlets from around the country. Museum leadership was also asked to participate in think tanks on the meaning of these symbols and monuments. The conversation was also taking place throughout Virginia and particularly in Richmond.

In the midst of these conversations, Virginia's GOP-controlled General Assembly quickly passed HB587 in March 2016 to expand protections of all war monuments with the specific intent to preserve Confederate-related monuments. The measure was designed to stop any attempt by localities to remove monuments or alter them in any way—including interpretive panels—an idea proposed by Richmond's cultural community. Fortunately, the Democratic governor, citing each community's right to determine what was best for it, vetoed the measure. Working closely with Governor Terry McAuliffe's administration and the Virginia Department of Historic and Natural Resources, the museum's leadership also advocated developing a tool kit for communities struggling with these very issues. The most important element of the tool kit was providing an array of resources to inform communities and decision-making. The official materials are slated for release in early 2017.

From the earliest institutions, it is clear Civil War history in particular is the confluence of history (what happened through document and artifact), heritage (what is passed through generations), and memory (personal experience with the past). It is not the creation of academics or museums, but rather negotiations among communities with their trusted institutions. However, museums can and should be powerful advocates for narrative change by engaging and challenging their communities to consider new research and the questions raised by it. Through it all, the experience of the American Civil War Museum and its predecessors demonstrate museums are powerful influencers in public history narratives.

Interpretation of the American Civil War is not for the weak of heart. It is relentless, but rewarding. It is work that must be done because at the heart of this history are the very things Americans of every background grapple with in contemporary times: appropriate balance of state versus federal powers, human and civil rights, enduring legacies of racism, and so forth. This history is not dead or past. This history is present. The American Civil War Museum continues its important work among the ruins.

Notes

1. "Civil War at 150: Still Relevant Still Divisive," Pew Research Center, US Politics and Policy, last modified April 8, 2011, http://www.people-press.org/2011/04/08/civil-War-at-150-still -relevant-still-divisive/.
2. "Preamble, Constitution of the Confederate States of America, March 11, 1861," *The Avalon Project*, accessed December 5, 2016. http://avalon.law.yale.edu/19th_century/csa_csa.asp.
3. Caroline E. Janney, "Ladies' Memorial Associations," *Encyclopedia Virginia*, last modified March 8, 2012, http://www.encyclopediavirginia.org/ladies_Memorial_Associations.
4. Venable's remarks quoted in *Organization of the Lee Monument Association: And the Association of the Army of Northern Virginia, Richmond, Va., November 3 & 4, 1870* (Richmond: JW Randolph & English, 1871), 19.
5. Stephen Weil, *Making Museums Matter* (Washington, DC: Smithsonian Books, 2002), 73.
6. "Open Season on General Lee," Virginia Division, United Daughters of the Confederacy, accessed December 10, 2016. http://vaudc.org/lee-torched.html.
7. Remarks by Dwight C. Jones delivered April 4, 2015, on steps of Virginia State Capital during keynote address.

CHAPTER 2

Billy Yank, not Johnny Reb

Focusing Civil War Exhibits on the Union in Virginia

Mark Benbow

THE CIVIL WAR IS A SUBJECT of intense interest in Virginia.[1] To anyone with a familiarity with public history this statement is about as controversial, and as obvious, as commenting upon the definitive wetness of water. The Museum of the Confederacy is in Richmond, as are numerous other museums devoted to the events of 1861–1865.[2] Much of the state is marked by battlefields, from Manassas to Petersburg, and throughout even the most remote small towns scattered through the state there are signs designating a spot as the site of fighting between Union and Confederate. According to the Virginia Department of Historic Resources database there are at least 699 historical markers (out of approximately 2,500) in the state devoted to the events of the war. Local historic societies celebrate and remember this period as well, often with artifacts from local figures who served in the war. In Virginia this seems to most often mean the focus is on Confederate soldiers, the artifacts lovingly preserved from someone who served in the gray rather than for the blue.[3]

One exception to this is the Arlington Historical Museum, operated by the Arlington Historical Society (AHS) in Arlington, Virginia, which may be the only local history museum in the state with an emphasis on the Union side of the war. There are no Confederate flags on display and the Civil War exhibits focus on the Union Army. This is not a result of recent controversies over the Confederate flag, although Arlington is not immune to debates over the public display of Confederate imagery. There have been recent discussions about renaming Washington-Lee High School (the county's oldest) and on renaming Jefferson Davis Highway. The county does not fly a Confederate flag over county buildings, and so has not seen the oft-heated debates over the flag and race seen elsewhere in the South. Situated on the very northern tip of the state, Arlington seems to be situated on the edge of the debate over displays of the Confederate flag.[4]

Despite the county seemingly being on the periphery of this debate there are, nonetheless, multiple ironies in the Arlington Historical Museum's emphasis upon the Union. The county was the home of Robert E. Lee. Indeed, the county is named after his estate. The museum is housed in a 1890s schoolhouse named after Frank Hume (1843–1906), who donated part of the land on which the school stands. Hume was a local businessman, landowner, and a Confederate veteran. Why then are the museum's displays on the war focused on the Union and not the Confederacy? Why does it not fit with the emphasis shared by the other museums in the state? The reasons lay in the history of the county before, during, and after the war. Arlington was Union territory during the Civil War, in sympathy as well as because it was occupied by Union troops. The exhibits reflect the complicated realities of regional loyalties during the war, which went beyond the simplistic South = Confederacy model that much of the public assumes. The exhibits in the Arlington Historical Museum attempt to correct this one-dimensional view of history. Moreover, this focus on the Union reflects the society's efforts to build closer ties to the county's African American community. Those efforts would be complicated by displays filled with Confederate imagery especially after events such as the 2015 murders at Charleston's Emanuel African Methodist Episcopal Church. In this case historical accuracy serves to make the museum more welcoming to a wider community.

Arlington County

Arlington County was not always a part of Virginia. It was included in the original boundaries of the District of Columbia. Known as Alexandria County until 1920, Arlington was often dominated by the much more populous Alexandria City, a relationship that sometimes took the county in a direction it did not wish to travel. For example, in the 1840s Alexandria City was an important slave-trading port and city leaders looked on with worry as abolitionists pressed Congress to eliminate the slave trade in the capital city. Should Congress agree to end the slave trade, Alexandria City's economy would suffer a disastrous setback. Already believing that the Virginia side of the District was being neglected economically, Alexandria's civic leaders lobbied both Congress and Richmond for retrocession. In July 1846 Congress agreed to return the southern portion of the District to Virginia pending a referendum. The city of Alexandria overwhelmingly voted in favor, 763 to 222, while Alexandria County voted just as overwhelmingly, against, 106 to 29. This was not the last time Alexandria City and Alexandria County differed in their relationship with the District of Columbia.[5]

From February 15 to April 4, 1861, the Virginia Convention debated secession. At first the delegates voted against leaving the Union, 90–45. On April 15, after Confederate forces fired on Fort Sumter, President Abraham Lincoln called for 75,000 volunteers to put down the rebellion. The Virginia Convention was still in session and Unionists found themselves rapidly losing support. This time the Convention voted in favor of secession, 88–55, to be confirmed in a statewide referendum on May 23. When the referendum was held, Virginians voted in favor of leaving the Union by an official vote of 132,201 to 37,451. These totals are suspect. Because it was not a secret ballot, in many places pro-Union men were threatened if they dared vote against secession. Nonetheless, while Alexandria City voted 925–81 in favor of secession, Alexandria County voted to remain in the Union 58–25. Some of this may have reflected the county's important economic ties to the District of Columbia. Another reason for the pro-Union sentiment was in part due to a large northern influence in the county. Much of the land in northern Virginia had been exhausted by tobacco farming. Many northerners had moved to Alexandria and Fairfax Counties to buy the land cheap, then revive it with modernized farming techniques. More modern agricultural techniques worked, and many of the transplanted northerners prospered. Much of the anti-secession vote presumably came from this group.[6]

Within hours of the vote, early on May 24, 1861, US troops landed in Alexandria City and marched across the bridges from DC into Alexandria County. As a result, this northern tip of Virginia was officially part of the Confederacy for less than a day. The US Army built an ever-growing series of forts, artillery batteries, rifle trenches, and Union camps around Washington to protect the capital. By April 1865, sixty-eight enclosed earthen forts ringed the city, along with over ninety supporting batteries and miles of rifle trenches. Thirty-three forts and twenty-five batteries were located south of the Potomac River. Between ten and twenty-five thousand men at a time served in these defenses. Alexandria County also hosted training camps, preparing soldiers in the Union's armies for fighting in and around Virginia, including the Army of the Potomac and the Army of the James. Alexandria County was for a few years the largest military base in the world.[7]

Despite tilting pro-Union, much of the local civilian population fled as soldiers moved into the area. Throughout northern Virginia, those who remained found it did not matter which side they supported, Union or Confederate. Soldiers from both armies would take whatever they needed from residents: food, livestock, timber, clothing, shoes, horses, and so on. Abandoned homes and barns became quarters for officers, hospitals, and stables, or would be torn down for lumber. Sometimes they'd simply be put to the torch to deny them to the enemy. Almost every large tree in the county was felled for fuel or lumber, or to provide a clear field of fire for artillery. Remaining civilians lived under tight security requirements, including carrying passes to move from one area to another. Of course, not everything was grim. Some did a booming business selling supplies to the military. A few local girls found sweethearts and husbands among the young men based in the county. Reviews and parades provided entertainment for the locals.[8]

When the war ended the soldiers went home and almost all of the forts were dismantled or abandoned, saving only Fort Whipple, which became Fort Myer. The wood and stone used in the forts were put to use by local residents on farms and in homes. Numerous relics were left behind, and as a result, unearthed objects are an important part of the Arlington Historic Museum's collection. The remains of a few parts of some of the forts have been preserved as local parks. A small corner of Fort Scott in south Arlington survives today, as well as part of Fort Ethan Allen in the northern part of the county. Nonetheless, most of the forts survive only in memory as names of local spots or as historic markers.

The county found itself in conflict with Richmond again during the civil rights era. Not that Arlington was an oasis of racial harmony. During the 1920s the Ku Klux Klan had an active chapter in the county, and Arlington faithfully followed the state's Jim Crow laws. Its schools were segregated, as was its housing. African American students who wanted to attend high school had to go to DC until the 1930s, when Arlington's all-black Hoffman Boston Junior High added a high school program. The African American Halls Hill neighborhood in north Arlington was segregated by a six-foot concrete brick wall, built without openings to separate it from the all-white Waycroft-Woodlawn development next door. Arlington was, nonetheless, one of the first counties in the state to integrate when, in 1959, four African American students began to attend the previously all-white Stratford Junior High. It was not until 1971 that the last segregated elementary schools were desegregated.[9]

The Arlington Historical Museum

This historic background shaped the redesign of the museum's exhibits. They had been neglected for some time, not out of malice or incompetence, but from a lack of resources. The museum opened in 1963 and eventually had exhibits on all three floors of the building (including the basement) and was open three days a week. The upper floor and basement display spaces became storage. The exhibits had become stale, and there were large gaps in the history being told as well. For example, there were few artifacts representing the local African American community. The Civil War was represented by one large case, one small one, and a couple of large free-standing objects.[10]

There was a great deal of potential, however. The collection contains some great Civil War artifacts such as a Union officer's sword dropped by its fleeing owner after First Bull Run. The question was how to best design new exhibits using what artifacts were already in the society's possession and how to locate the resources needed to display them. The Arlington Historical Society, unlike the other local history societies in the area, gets no county funds. It relies on returns from small investments, membership dues, an annual fundraiser held by a local woman's club, and a year-end fundraising campaign by the society. Moreover, there is a small accession budget using funds from the sale a few years before of unneeded items. As a result, new displays would have to be created on a limited budget, and, if possible, use more of what was already in the collection.

The Civil War cases currently take up the largest amount of space for any one event or period. The single largest case needed few changes, keeping the collection of Minié balls, a Union artillery jacket, the Union sword, and small items found by local archeologists. The case also includes several *Harper's Weekly* pages with illustrations of the local forts. Other objects were pulled out of storage, including a model built for the Civil War centennial in the early 1960s of a local lunette-style fort. It had deteriorated in storage and was unusable. An intern restored the model, adding appropriately scaled artillery pieces and men. Next to it is a smaller case with various artillery shells, cannon balls, and shrapnel found in the county.

Two large objects presented more difficulties: the "Jefferson Davis Desk" and the Civil War tombstone. A local family donated the desk to the museum in 1967. According to family lore the desk originally came from Thomas Jefferson's Monticello. Jefferson Davis used it during the war, and it was on this desk that he wrote his rejection of President Abraham Lincoln's offer to let the Confederate leader propose his own terms to end the war. After the war the desk was given to a family member. There was a sworn notarized statement from 1968 attesting to the story.

There were several problems with this family legend, the most important of which was that Lincoln never made such an offer to Davis. There was also the issue of whether the desk belonged to Davis at all, even without the Lincoln story. The society contacted the Confederate White House in Richmond, and they replied that they had no knowledge of such a desk, or of one being given as a gift. Monticello informed the AHS that there was no record of a desk from there being given to Jefferson Davis, but they did say that the desk was of a type made before the Civil War.

How to handle this artifact? The desk is interesting for guests interested in antique furniture, and visitors often ask about it. The family story was untrue, so the display could not repeat it as accurate. However, the family had given the desk to the AHS in good faith and clearly believed the legend. Such myths are important to families as a way to remember a part of their history. Striking a balance between the legend and what facts could be documented, the resulting display card is worded thus:

The "Jefferson Davis Desk."
Donated to the Arlington Historical Society by the Herbert Carter family in 1967. According to a family legend, the desk was given to Fred Sickles by Jefferson Davis at an unknown date. The desk was reportedly made from walnut from Thomas Jefferson's Monticello estate. It was saved from a fire in 1924 and kept in the family until it was donated to the museum. Unfortunately there is no documentation to support the family story and inquiries with museums in Richmond and elsewhere have failed to find any evidence to verify that the desk ever belonged to Jefferson Davis. This is not unusual. Family stories often change over time as details are forgotten or embellished. However, even if family stories cannot be verified, historical artifacts represent a portion of a family's history and how the family wishes to remember that history. Such stories are an important part of how the Civil War is remembered in American society. Whether or not the desk belonged to Confederate President Jefferson Davis, the family preserved the desk as a memorial to their ancestor, and to remember an important event in their family's history.

The focus of the desk as an object now is not the apocryphal connection to Davis, but the importance to families of how they remember their history. Using the object as a lesson on memory avoids repeating the story as true, but gives it a significance to local history. It also illustrates how, despite the county's Union leanings during the war, there were Confederate sympathizers as well. Like other communities around the south, Arlington was divided. The difference with most of the rest of the state is that the Unionists were the majority faction.

Figure 2.1. The Robert Jones marker, the "Jefferson Davis Desk," and "Billy." Photo by Mark Benbow

The Confederate tombstone was another difficult object to interpret because it has little documentation. Made of marble, it is about four feet tall and very heavy. It had been donated to the AHS in 1981 by the Arlington Police Department where it had reportedly been used as a rather large doorstop. Matching the Confederate gravestone style of the markers at Arlington National Cemetery, it was engraved for Robert S. Jones, a Confederate soldier who died in 1863. Oddly, he is not buried in Arlington nor did he participate in any of the small skirmishes fought in the county. The only local connection was that he had a tombstone made for the national cemetery and that it was found in the local police department. Despite this, the tombstone was worth displaying. The museum had little representing Arlington National Cemetery on display and it was unlikely the collection could acquire another genuine marker. As with the desk, the display card for the stone marker was worded carefully:

The Search for Robert S. Jones.

In 1981 the Arlington police discovered this tombstone of Robert S. Jones being used as a doorstop and brought it to the museum. With a peaked top, it was made in the style used to mark the graves of Confederate soldiers in Arlington National Cemetery. Markers for Union veterans have a curved top. The height of the stone allows it to be buried deep enough that the stone will continue to stand upright as the years pass. Footing the stone deep within the earth also prevents vandalism and souvenir-hunting.

Who was Robert S. Jones? In 1860 Robert was 17 years old and lived with his brothers, sisters, and Mother, Martha Jones, in Greensville County in southeastern Virginia. One year later he enlisted in Company F of the 12th Virginia Calvary stationed in Norfolk. A transfer to Company I where his brother Richard was captain followed and Robert took part in the defense of Richmond. On June 9, 1862 he was one of 34 members of his company wounded in the Battle of Seven Pines where Confederates checked General George C. McClellan's advance on Richmond. Furloughed home and declared unfit for active duty, Robert requested permission to serve as a recruiting agent in Wilmont, North Carolina. Jones died at home on July 11, 1863, of "disease." It is believed that Robert was buried in his home community. How his tombstone came to Arlington is still an unanswered question.

The marker focuses first on the local connection, its designed function as a grave marker in the national cemetery. It then shifts to the life of the young soldier for whom it was made. Rather than speculate on its origins the text simply noted it was a "mystery." Visitors often pause and read the display card and then call over other members of their group to see it, so it strikes some sort of chord with those who come to the museum.[11]

There were no real battles in the county, only a few skirmishes early on when the boundary between Union- and Confederate-held territories was rather fluid. As a result, the focus of the Civil War exhibits had to take a different tack than displays in museums elsewhere in the state. The "Yankee invasion" was short and not especially violent since it consisted of men marching over bridges and taking up positions. There was some bloodshed in Alexandria City, where US Army Colonel Elmer E. Ellsworth was shot and killed by secessionist hotel owner James W. Jackson after the colonel removed a huge Confederate flag from atop Jackson's hotel. Jackson was shot and killed by Ellsworth's men. There is still a plaque on the hotel building celebrating Jackson as "first martyr to the cause of Southern Independence." It makes no mention of Ellsworth.[12]

This plaque marks one of the key differences between Alexandria City and Arlington County. As noted earlier, the city voted for secession while the county voted against. Their remembrance of the war remains different as well. Alexandria City's historic memory for the Civil War period remains largely focused on the Confederacy, although they do house a restored Union fortification, Fort Ward. There is still debate on moving a statue of a Confederate soldier placed with his back to Washington. Placed on the major north-south street in the city, it now blocks a major commuting thoroughfare. Whenever someone suggests moving it, however, enough residents, including a local chapter of the United Daughters of the Confederacy, complain bitterly that it remains in its spot. The soldier's back is turned toward DC, which now fortuitously faces him against traffic so that he cannot see the rude gestures made by frustrated commuters. Finally, while there are no chapters of the Sons of Confederate Veterans in Arlington, there are two in Alexandria and one in neighboring Fairfax County.[13]

While Alexandria still remembers its occupation by Union troops, Arlington County's Civil War memory focuses largely but not exclusively on the Union presence. There is also a powerful tie to the memory of Robert E. Lee and Arlington House. Besides the roads and school named after him, Lee's Arlington home is the most prominent monument to his memory in the county and, along with the national cemetery, is still the county's biggest tourist attraction. Indeed, the county seal used until 2007 featured the front of Arlington House. It was replaced by a more stylized design of the same building, which is not as easily recognized. The Civil War sesquicentennial, however, sparked a new interest in the Union forts and the troops manning them. In 2014 the county paid for preservation of the remains of Fort Ethan Allen, including clearing brush so visitors could see the remaining works, adding several historic markers, and even placing a replica Civil War–era cannon pointed at the bedroom of a suburban house across the street.

The AHS took advantage of this interest to expand the museum's coverage of the events of 1861–1865 with an exhibit on the men of the forts. The impetus for this exhibit came in early 2013 from a local man who had three original photographs of one of his ancestors in his Union uniform, and a letter to the young man from his hometown sweetheart back in Massachusetts. In August 1864 John W. Bates had enlisted in the 23rd US Army Massachusetts Volunteers, one of fourteen companies of heavy artillery raised that month throughout Massachusetts for a one-year term. Bates was in Company G of the 4th Regiment, which spent its entire year of service on garrison duty in the defenses of Washington south of the Potomac until it was mustered out on June 17, 1865. Entering service as a private, Bates was promoted to Second Lieutenant on August 23, 1864.[14]

The local descendent had the three photographs of Bates from the war, as well as photos of him as an older man, one of a store he ran after the war, and a letter from his future wife. The three images of Bates in uniform were a wonderful way to show a Union soldier that was stationed in the county. The letter from his sweetheart Nancie (sic) was loving and chatty about news from their home in East Weymouth. The frost had killed the beans, a neighbor had a new horse, and a local business had raised an eighteen-foot American flag. Nancie also shared how much she missed John: "The beautiful days of autumn are here, with their lucid mornings and quiet evenings. This week I walked down that street you and I used to go to enjoy each other's company. I only wished you were with me."[15]

The response was gratifying. People came to the museum specifically to see the exhibit and visitors asked questions about life for the Union soldiers in the local forts. A local library branch asked the AHS to put up a temporary exhibit on life in the forts in their display cases. The society's annual journal included an article on soldiers' lives in the forts, and a local magazine published a less scholarly version for its general audience. It was clear this topic was of interest to local residents. The museum needed a permanent exhibit on life in the Union forts.[16]

A permanent display on Union forts features photographs, letters, and items that reflected the common soldier's day-to-day life, including coins, utensils, buttons, buckles and hooks, and even harmonica parts. EBay provided several letters from soldiers stationed in the county, and a society member purchased an original photo of an Ohio Union officer who served a short enlistment in the county's fortifications as well. Finally, the display features some bricks from the site of Fort Scott. The resulting exhibit shows how the Union soldiers ate, rested, trained, entertained themselves, and dealt with the locals. It also reinforces the fact that the county sided with DC during the war, not Richmond.

There are four cases on the Civil War, plus the desk and tombstone. The focus remains on the forts and soldiers living in them during the war and not specific battles. The only Confederate items are postwar: the tombstone representing the cemetery, and the desk, which illustrates the area's memory of the war. In addition, the basement houses a huge iron pot that a local resident used as a cook in the Confederate military. It is too heavy to be placed anywhere but on the basement floor. As a result, other than the desk and the tombstone the rest of the objects visitors can see are all oriented toward the Union. Is this a problem for the museum? How have people reacted?

Every year the society rents a booth for the county fair. Arlington is the smallest county in the country, so all the exhibits fit into a middle school gymnasium. However, while the fair is tiny, many come to enjoy the rides, eat deep-fried everything, play games to win small stuffed animals, and visit local organizations' booths. From 2011 through 2015 the

Figure 2.2. The model of a lunette-style fort (right) and the case displaying artifacts from the county's Union forts (left). Photo by Mark Benbow

AHS partnered with the county's Civil War Sesquicentennial Committee for a combined booth. The committee brought a small case of objects, both Union and Confederate, from a local collector. Unfortunately, most people just walked past without looking at the objects. Arlington is a very diverse community and it seemed as if Hispanic and Asian residents in particular just walked past without stopping. To capture visitors' eyes the booth needed something that would grab their attention, something that kids especially might enjoy.

The answer was a life-sized cut-out of a Union soldier named, somewhat unoriginally, "Billy." Visitors could stand behind a cutout face and have their photo taken as if they were a Union soldier. It immediately caught people's attention. Children and teens began to stop and pose while their parents and friends took photos. They often paused to look at the other material. Few complained that Billy was Union not Confederate but if they asked why the AHS chose that soldier, the volunteers manning the booth explained about the forts and how the county voted against secession. Most of those who asked were not aware of that part of the county's history. As far as the general public was concerned, Arlington was in Virginia, Virginia was Confederate, and therefore Arlington must have been so as well.[17]

It is this misperception that the AHS exhibits are designed to correct, both at the fair and at the museum. Historians of the Civil War know that taking sides during the war was far more complicated than mere geography. Large areas of the Confederacy were pro-Union. Most of the visitors over the past few years seem to accept this without too much argument.

Relations With the Local African American Community

There is another factor at play here, the AHS's relationship with the local African American community. The society was never deliberately segregated, but over the years had limited participation with persons of color. There was a local group trying to start an African American museum for the community and both they and the AHS shared members on their respective boards of directors. The museum acquired a few objects from local prominent black families, but the ties were limited to those established by a few individuals. However, the AHS has been trying to widen the appeal of the museum and to make it more representative of the county's history. Sometimes this involved subtle changes. In 2009 the AHS stopped using its original logo. Adopted in 1960 it featured Arlington House with a series of five flags representing those that flew over the county during its history. Four of the five were Confederate: the battle flag, and three different national flags. This was not only historically inaccurate, since the county was never really controlled by Richmond's government, but the flag's history as a symbol of resistance to the civil rights movement gave it strong negative connotations for many African Americans. The AHS logo was replaced with a stylized "Arlington."[18]

As a former school the museum has a model classroom set up that has caused a few issues regarding race and history as well. Hume School was all-white. It closed in the mid-1950s before the county schools integrated. Arranged to look like a classroom about 1900, it has on the wall not only a copy of the Declaration of Independence and a portrait of George Washington, but a portrait of General Lee. Moreover, there are a few old textbooks set around for kids to examine. They were in place for years before a black parent quietly pointed out some racist images, "Sambo"-like figures mostly, in some of the books. Similarly racist pictures of East Asians and Native Americans were in some of the texts as well. The books are no longer in the classroom, although they remain in the collection.

New exhibits now tell the story of Arlington's black community. In late 2016 the museum hosted an exhibit on the 150th Anniversary of a local African Methodist Episcopal church. Founded in 1866 in Freedman's Village, it is a long-established part of the historic African American community of Nauck in south Arlington. The AHS hosted the church's members for an opening reception, which attracted perhaps the largest crowd to the museum in memory. Multiple guests thanked the society for including their community's story at long last. There is also a large display case with a new permanent exhibit on local black history focusing on prominent people and on desegregation. Moreover, the society sponsors monthly speaker programs with local historians, often amateurs, to talk about a local history topic, including African American history. As a result, program audiences and museum visitors are beginning to be a bit more diverse and representative of the whole community.[19]

How do the Civil War exhibits fit into this effort? It would be more difficult to find an African American audience if the museum featured exhibits full of Confederate flags and displays lionizing General Lee or Stonewall Jackson. Certainly not every Union soldier based in Arlington was an abolitionist carrying a copy of *The Liberator* in his pack. But because Arlington was Union territory, slaves from around the region fled there to be liberated and to start their new lives as free men and women. That is a far more positive historical memory for the local African American community than displays of the Confederate flag, and it is more historically accurate.

Conclusion

The museum still has more to do to better tell the county's story. There is nothing on slavery in the county as yet, although the society hopes to acquire some objects such as slave shackles to add to the "Age of Custis" Antebellum case. It currently displays mostly material from some of the grand mansions that stood in the county. It would be more balanced and more complete to include the laborers who built those grand structures. The museum still needs material about the life of civilians in the county during the Civil War including Freedman's Village. Placing Arlington's history within the context of the Civil War, and getting beyond the simple Virginia equals Confederate myth is a large part of that restructuring and refocusing. It has made the museum more welcoming to a wider, more diverse group of residents while simultaneously improving the historic accuracy of the exhibits. It has also helped the Arlington Historical Society's efforts to build links to the county's African American community, ties long neglected. It's possible that in the future a visitor may complain of "political correctness," but expanding the stories told by the exhibit to include all of the community's members and to accurately portray the county's history during the Civil War adds to its historical correctness. It does make the museum more welcoming to more people, and what museum, outside of some of the huge Smithsonian's on the National Mall, would not love to have more visitors? Certainly, however, ever refining and improving its accuracy should be the goal of every person responsible for a history museum. Hopefully, the Arlington Historical Museum positively reflects that goal.

Notes

1. The views expressed in this chapter are those of the author and not necessarily those of the Arlington Historical Society or Marymount University.
2. The Museum of the Confederacy is now part of the American Civil War Museum in Richmond.
3. "Virginia Historical Highway Markers," *Virginia Department of Historic*, accessed November 6, 2016. http://www.dhr.virginia.gov/hiway_markers/hwmarker_info.htm. These numbers should be taken as approximate. They are based on a simple search for "Civil War." Unfortunately, the database search is very basic, so you cannot run searches on multiple terms at once to eliminate duplicates. This number represents markers with either the phrase "Civil War" or "War Between the States." There are five markers with the latter phrase.
4. The high school is unlikely to be renamed. Founded in 1924, it has always been named after both men. Moreover, both George Washington and Robert E. Lee were from the area so their names carry an even greater amount of weight than normal. There is more support for renaming Jefferson Davis Highway. The Confederate president was, after all, from Mississippi, not Virginia. However, the state legislature in Richmond controls the naming rights to the section of the highway in Arlington and they are generally unsympathetic to removing Confederate names.
5. Mitch Kachum, "Celebrating Emancipation and Contesting Freedom in Washington, D.C." *In the Shadow of Freedom: The Politics of Slavery in the National Capital*, Paul Finkleman and Donald R. Kennon, eds. (Athens: Ohio University Press, 2011), 223; the Virginia side was also at a disadvantage in economic development, which was heavily concentrated on the Maryland side of the river. For the election results see "Correspondence," *The Columbian Fountain* (Washington, DC) September 5, 1846, 2.
6. "The Election Yesterday," *Alexandria Gazette*, May 24, 1861, 1. They reported the total vote for Alexandria, including the county section, as 983–106 in favor. The breakdown by district, however, shows the division as the county was district #5, the only one of the five districts to vote against. The Southern Claims Commission files contain details about the vote as county residents applying for reimbursement for losses during the war (usually material taken by Union troops) testified about pressure from local secessionists to either vote for the Ordinance of Secession or to abstain. See, for example, those quoted in Ruth Ward, "Life in Alexandria County During the War," *The Arlington Historical Magazine* 7:4 (1984), 3–21; Richard H. Abbott, "Yankee Farmers in Northern Virginia, 1840–1860," *The Virginia Magazine of History and Biography* 76:1 (1968): 56–63.
7. Benjamin Franklin Cooling III and Walton H. Owen, II. *Mr. Lincoln's Forts: A Guide to the Civil War Defenses of Washington* (Lanham, MD: Scarecrow Press, 2010), xi; C. B. Rose Jr., "Civil War Forts in Arlington," *The Arlington Historical Magazine* 1:4 (1960): 19.
8. For details of the plight of civilians in the area, see Noel G. Harrison, "Atop an Anvil: The Civilians' War in Fairfax and Alexandria Counties, April 1861–April, 1862," *The Virginia Magazine of History and Biography* 106:2 (Spring 1998): 133–64. After the war, the Southern Claims Commission was established to review claims by Unionist southerners for losses

suffered through the actions of Union troops. Several Arlington residents filed claims. Ruth Ward, "Life in Alexandria County during the Civil War," *The Arlington Historical Magazine* 7:4 (October 1884).

9. Klavern No. 6 met in Ballston, and was even listed in the local phone book. Janet Wamsley, "The K.K.K. in Arlington in the 1920s," *The Arlington Historical Magazine* 10:1 (1993): 55–59; Steve Vogel, *The Pentagon: A History* (New York: Random House, 2008), 203–205; John Liebertz, "Segregation Wall," *A Guide to the African-American Heritage of Arlington County, Virginia* (Arlington: Department of Community Planning, Housing and Development, Historic Preservation Program, 2016), 22. The wall still stands today, although with openings for cars and pedestrians, and both neighborhoods are integrated; Cecelia Michelotti, "Arlington School Desegregation: A History," *The Arlington Historical Magazine* 8:4 (1988), 5–20; David Dexter, "Integration with a Minimum of Integration," Virginia Center for Digital History (2005).

10. L. L. Ecker-Racz, "How the Hume School Historical Museum Happened," *The Arlington Historical Magazine* 2:3 (1963): 14; Kathryn Holt, "The Arlington Historical Museum," *Northern Virginia Heritage* 7:2 (June 1985): 15–17. Turning the second floor and basement from display space to storage may also be related to their not being ADA compliant, although as an older structure, the museum could have been grandfathered in.

11. A mystic chord of memory perhaps.

12. George G. Kundahl, *Alexandria Goes To War: Beyond Robert E. Lee* (Knoxville: University of Tennessee Press, 2004), 15, 305.

13. I have been on the ghost tour multiple times taking my public history class. Besides describing the killer as a "Yankee carpetbagger," I have also heard him described as an Englishman who moved to Alexandria in the late eighteenth century. In both cases, carpetbagger and Englishman, the killer was cast as an outsider. Moreover, just a few years ago one of my public history students, an Alexandria City native with deep family roots in the city, wrote in a term paper, "Even though it was occupied by the enemy, true Alexandrians considered themselves Confederates."

14. Bates's record of service is listed in *Massachusetts Soldiers, Sailors and Marines in the Civil War* (Norwood, MA: Norwood Press, 1933), 34. Other documentation is included in the records of the National Archives. M. Wesley Clark, one of Bates's descendants, provided copies to me. Assigned to Fort Blenker, the 23rd lost two officers and twenty-three enlisted men to disease during the war.

15. Nancie (LNU) to Lt. John W. Bates, October 11, 1864. Copy in author's possession.

16. Mark Benbow, "Camp Life for Union Soldiers in Arlington," *The Arlington Historical Magazine* (October 2013): 6–17; Mark Benbow, "Holding the Line," *Arlington Magazine* (November–December 2013).

17. According to the 2010 census Arlington is about 64 percent white, 9 percent black, 10 percent Asian, and 15 percent Hispanic or Latino.

18. It was designed by Lt. Colonel Henry Leon Taylor of Arlington, Virginia. "The Society's Seal," *The Arlington Historical Magazine* 1:4 (1960): 59–60.

19. Programs have featured other communities as well, including Vietnamese. The county has a large Southeast Asian community dating from the fall of South Vietnam in 1975.

CHAPTER 3

A Civil War Museum in Kenosha, Wisconsin?

Daniel Joyce, Douglas Dammann,

Jennifer Edginton

" "A CIVIL WAR MUSEUM in Wisconsin? Really?" "But there weren't any battles nearby!" "Did anyone from [insert Upper Midwest state name here] even serve during the war?" "Was Wisconsin even a state back then?"

These are all questions the staff at The Civil War Museum in Kenosha, Wisconsin, regularly field. While some people might interpret these queries negatively, we see them as positive, teachable moments. Each question presents an opportunity to educate visitors about the Civil War history of the Upper Middle West and what makes our region's experiences unique to that narrative. Visitors are often amazed to learn that our key focus region (Illinois, Indiana, Iowa, Wisconsin, Michigan, Minnesota, and Ohio) not only were indeed states in 1861, but sent more than one million men off to war.

For some, a visit to The Civil War Museum is the first time they realize their own family and community connection to the war, and that their ancestors played an important role in one of the largest and most pivotal events in American history. Armed with this knowledge, they leave feeling a greater kinship with the settlers and immigrants who came to the Upper Midwest. The visitors understand what they did and that these people were very much like us, not a relic of the distant past.

Origin

On the face of it, many might not view Kenosha, located between Chicago and Milwaukee, as the ideal location for a Civil War museum. But this unlikely location, far from the more famous Civil War battlefields, freed staff to consider a view of the war from a different perspective. The Civil War Museum started as a simple story that begged expansion: that of the famed Iron Brigade, the only all-Western brigade in the Army of the Potomac. Made up of three regiments from Wisconsin, Indiana, and Michigan, the Iron Brigade became one of the most recognized units in the war. It was Kenosha Mayor John Antaramian who initially proposed the idea of a museum dedicated to the Iron Brigade.

In 2004, to develop a better idea of how museums and historic sites were interpreting the Civil War, eight staff, board, and city officials visited nineteen Civil War–related monuments, sites, museums, and battlefield visitor centers. We discovered that of those we visited, only four museums (National Civil War Museum, National Museum of the Civil War Soldier, National Museum of Civil War Medicine, Museum of the Confederacy) dealt with all four years of the war. Many battlefield visitor center museums focused on their battle. Other museums had a special focus, such as Civil War medicine. During our travels, we encountered sites with older exhibits featuring rows of muskets and limited interpretation. We knew we wanted to offer something different. At our very first meeting with historian Lance Herdegen, he suggested that the contributions made by the Upper Midwest should be our big story and we were centrally located to this oft-overlooked history.

Historians, Civil War buffs, and the general public often largely define the Civil War in more military terms: soldiers, combat, and battles. The war is about more—men, women, and children both at the front and at home. The story is rich and more than military history alone. The average visitor to a military museum is often overwhelmed by blow-by-blow accounts of battle after battle. They do not relate to the movements of entire armies. They become disengaged. In order to engage a wider audience, our approach was to tell stories about men, women, and children, a social history that tells individual tales of ordinary Midwestern soldiers and home front families in extraordinary times. Visitors relate better to individuals. You cannot easily develop empathy when discussing the tactical movements of thousands of men. We present these stories through the eyes of Midwesterners, set in a broader historical context. The Civil War Museum immerses visitors in "you are there" exhibits that carry them through an expansive history of the Upper Midwest, from the buildup to the war, through the four years that tore the nation apart, to its long-lasting aftermath, which affects our country to this day.

The tremendous amount of uncensored, primary source material available for the Civil War is staggering. All through the exhibits our labels are the familiar format of "daily newspapers" with themed headlines and stories supported by period illustrations, political cartoons, excerpts from diaries and letters, maps, and advertisements. Sub-headed articles allow the visitors to pick and choose the portion of a label that interests them most.

The Fiery Trial Exhibit: Build-up to War

We will walk through the main exhibit, "The Fiery Trial," to illustrate the varied immersive methods used to present the Midwest in the Civil War. As visitors enter the exhibit, they are surrounded by Civil War tombstones in a Midwestern cemetery, and Civil War statues and cannons in Midwestern parks. Floor-to-ceiling murals set the scene. Each day, we rush by these relics of the past and pay little attention. Starting with a contemporary perspective, we make the war a part of our visitors' life today and as a result they become invested and want to learn more. From this introduction visitors turn a corner to travel back to 1850 when the Upper Midwest was young and part of an expanding nation. They encounter the story of a new frontier, the "West" of its day. It's a story made of the experiences of men, women, and children of the Upper Midwest. What follows is a heterogeneous tale about Native Americans (Wisconsin has the largest population east of the Mississippi River), new settlers from the East and South, European immigrants, free African Americans, escaped slaves, abolitionists, and the Underground Railroad.

Our aspiration was to emphasize to our audience that these people were more than dusty, two-dimensional, sepia-toned images. They were people just like them: with hopes and dreams, prejudices and fears. The goal of any history museum is to bring the people of the past to life. After all, history is made up of stories about people. In our rush to present the facts of history we, as historians, sometimes forget this fact. It is easy to lose the personal thread when speaking about the movements of thousands of men on a battlefield. Our job in presenting history is to present it in a way that will be understood by our visitors, not just by our peers. We knew that we could not afford to narrow our audience.

Developing empathy for persons in our past is one of the more difficult but essential things that we do in the museum field. Since our medium is not book length, we cannot evoke empathy the way a novelist is able to through tens of thousands of words. We have a minimum of words. It is similar to writing a book for young children. For a children's book, the words are minimal and the supporting illustrations bring people to life. In the case of museum exhibitions, the supporting material is made up of photos, graphics, audio, video, and artifacts. Our visitors each carry very different perspectives into the exhibit, but by bringing a historical figure to life and creating empathy for that figure, we create a memorable experience. This makes history meaningful and interesting to our audience.

Three simple push button stations allow visitors to follow twelve individuals before, during, and after the war. You can follow a farm girl, an Irish immigrant, a Native American, or an escaped slave. You can see what happened to them, explore their feelings, beliefs, and fate. In addition to humanizing the participants in the war, this also illustrates how integral and important the Midwest was in the Civil War.

Further along, as visitors navigate from a rural homestead to a typical Midwestern town, they get closer to the people and flow of events leading up to the war. Artifacts, the aforementioned "daily newspapers," and audio trips allow you to overhear conversations that raise the issues of the day in a personal way. Since the area was a hotbed of abolitionists and the western end of the Underground Railroad, how did Midwesterners feel about slavery and the Fugitive Slave Act that made everyone in northern states a de facto slave catcher? In one overheard conversation a wife chides her husband for hiding an escaped slave in the barn and putting the family in danger of arrest. How did Midwesterners feel as increasing sectional conflicts led to war? In another overheard conversation men debate whether Southerners will fight. In many instances, the views of Upper Midwesterners were as mixed as the rest of the country. Illinois, for example, provides an interesting case. The southern region of the state had close ancestral and business ties with Kentucky, Tennessee, and Missouri. The northern region was populated by settlers from New York, Ohio, and

Pennsylvania along with immigrants from Western Europe. In the end, the state's northern regions voted for the Republican Abraham Lincoln for president; its southern half voted Democratic. The people of the Upper Midwest were every bit as engaged as the rest of the country because the controversies leading up to the war were taking place all around them. At every turn, you can see that the issues that were tearing apart the nation were just as important in the Midwest as they were in the East and South.

At the Front

Telling stories in a museum today is both daunting and exciting. New technology offers many techniques that can lead to great success or expensive failure. In the Fiery Trial exhibit, visitors board a "moving" train and sit next to mannequins that tell distinctly Midwestern stories. Here you learn about why they are on the move in 1861. Men are leaving to become officers; women going east to become nurses to their sick and injured husbands, brothers, or sons; and other wives and children stay behind to run family farms and businesses. The train vibrates, the landscape passes by, and our visitors interact with people on the move, learning in a unique way how the war impacted Midwesterners. It is by far the favorite part of the exhibit for families.

As visitors leave the train they arrive at the battle front. Here they learn how new Midwestern recruits adapted to military life. They learn what soldiers ate, how they coped with the boredom of camp life, how they endured winter, the importance of mail and packages from loved ones, and medical practices, among other things. They discover that combat was a significant, but small portion of the overall soldier experience and that disease was ever present.

Our visitors do not learn about any specific battle but do experience the impact battle had on the men. Effective communication in museums does not allow for in-depth minutiae. It is not that this information is unimportant, but it can easily be accessed via many excellent books, Internet sites, or by visiting the actual battlefields. Our decision was to concentrate on the personal experience of battle.

Visitors also learn that the Upper Midwest, often perceived as being distant from military action, found itself in the middle of armed conflict. The North's supply depot at Cairo, at the southern tip of Illinois, is actually farther south than the Confederate capital city of Richmond. Conflict-torn Missouri extends halfway up the western side of Illinois. Only the Mississippi and Ohio Rivers separated Illinois from the front in Missouri and Kentucky. Small Confederate raids struck into Ohio, Indiana, and Iowa—three of our core Midwestern states.

In 1862, the Dakota Indian uprising created a second front and spread fear throughout Minnesota, extending to neighboring Wisconsin. Although the conflict was localized, these fears were real to them, as the populations of both states contained a significant number of Native Americans. This event signaled the beginning of the long, sustained postwar, westward expansion onto Native lands, and the final conflict with Native Americans that influences government policy to this day.

Figure 3.1. At the outbreak of war the visitor can board a train, sit next to an Upper Midwesterner, and hear a one-minute audio presentation telling about why they are on the move at the beginning of the war. The train rumbles as the scenery passes by. This is one of many ways in which information is presented to the visitor. The Civil War Museum, Kenosha, Wisconsin

"Seeing the Elephant" in 360°

We believe that to effectively tell stories, you need to engage your visitor on as many levels as possible, taking advantage of individual learning styles. A circular room central to the Fiery Trial exhibit tells of each state's contribution at the front, and the battle-related stories unique to those states. One of our first ideas was to present a twenty-first-century update of the late-nineteenth-century Civil War cyclorama paintings. We wanted to present a historically accurate, multisensory, ten-minute film that portrays the nature of Civil War training and skirmish combat. The producers of the film recorded the realities of camp and battle with 360-degree digital camera technology. More than two hundred people, including actors, reenactors, film crew, technical and historical advisers, and museum staff, gathered for a five-day shoot for what became *Seeing the Elephant*. The film is shown on an eleven-foot-tall, 140-foot-around screen that completely encircles visitors. Visitors view the movie from a raised central platform. This raised platform directs the visitor's eye so that the screen surrounds them, immersing them in the film. Eight projected moving images are stitched into one seamless in-the-round experience. The floor shakes, directional speakers highlight action points, and light fixtures change color throughout the presentation to help transition scene changes and assist visitors in following the story line.

In *Seeing the Elephant*, we sought to depict a skirmish experience as honestly as possible. We did not want to make a film that was ineffective, cliché, or a duplicate of first-person battle action video games. We also did not want to do something to dishonor the experience of these men in combat. The goal of this skirmish experience was to bring those stoic two-dimensional people's combat experiences to life and give the visitor a small glimpse of what it is like to stand shoulder to shoulder in battle. Quotes from primary sources were utilized as the basis for the script to give an authentic voice and help visitors realize that a Civil War soldier was like them, someone's son, husband, father, or brother.

The movie follows three soldiers from very different backgrounds, each with his own reasons for enlisting: one to help preserve the Union, another for adventure, and the third for his abolitionist beliefs. It follows them from enlistment, through the boredom of camp life, fear the war would be over before they could do their part, life on the front lines, the reality of battle, and ultimately dealing with the war's lasting consequences. The movie tells a sad but realistic story and helps the visitor connect with how the war affected the men and their families. Reactions to the film reflect a wide range of emotions. Combat veterans have praised the film as accurately portraying the life of a soldier and the chaos and emotions of battle.

Visitors enter an area to reflect on the lives and challenges that Civil War veterans and their families faced in the decades after the war. Leaving the front, they board a paddle wheel steamer bound for home. Lincoln has been assassinated and some of the same people that you saw on the train, you meet again as they tell you what happened in the intervening four years. Disembarking, you enter the same town that you left four years earlier, but it is different. It is draped in mourning for the Midwest's fallen president, but the old dirt streets are now cobblestone, telegraph poles are evident and brick houses predominate, all telling of an economic boom during the war. But there are costs, the dead being shipped home, the reconstruction of a nation, the orphans and the war veterans that need care. As time passes, the Grand Army of the Republic is founded and has considerable influence over the next fifty years of politics. They start to build monuments to the war and reflect on their wartime experiences. By 1900 the war is a dimmer memory that still has a hold on the country.

Lasting Effects

In the last portion of the Fiery Trial exhibit is *The Enduring Civil War*. Visitors leave the immersive exhibit and enter a small changing transition space that explores the ways the war remains relevant today in the form of civil rights issues, the Ku Klux Klan, Confederate flag controversies, and in popular novels and movies. Next they find themselves back where they began their visit, standing among Civil War tombstones, statues, and cannons. Now they have a better understanding and appreciation for these monuments that they pass everyday.

School Programs

For museums in closer proximity to major battlefields, it is less difficult to emphasize the war's impact on the region. The Civil War is all around them, directly confronting them at every turn. In the absence of this geographic connection, it is a greater challenge to convince visitors of the impact of the war on the people of the Midwest region. However, for the Civil

Figure 3.2. Immersive dioramas, ambient background audio, overheard conversations, photo murals, and nearby artifact cases all set the scene and engage multiple senses, developing empathy for our ancestors. The Civil War Museum, Kenosha, Wisconsin

War Museum's school group programming, the location of the museum is an advantage. The museum offers teachers a way to help students gain a better understanding of how important the region was to the war effort, and can make that all-important personal, local connection to its history and aftermath. Teachers have expressed that too often, textbooks and resources they use include very little about troops from their home states, instead concentrating on the more popular and well-known battles fought in the Eastern Theater. This gives many students the wrong impression that Midwestern states did little to contribute. As one teacher commented in her written evaluation of their visit, "We cover the Civil War from a national perspective, that's why your museum is so great, it brings it to the regional level." Presenting the larger war in a regional context not only engages them, it makes the Civil War more relevant and real to them.

For middle and high school students, we developed a tour, Midwest in the Civil War, as a framework for their visit. In it, staff and volunteers use the region's history to teach students about the Civil War. It focuses on three major themes: soldiers, food, and natural resources.

The first theme, soldiers, emphasizes that 49 percent of the Union Army came from the Upper Midwest. Equally important for school groups is to highlight the diversity of the soldiers in these regiments. Units comprised immigrants from Germany, Norway, and Ireland; American-born settlers from New England, upstate New York, and the South; Native Americans from tribes like the Ojibwa of the Great Lakes region; and escaped slaves and free African Americans who called the Midwest home before joining regiments like the 29th United States Colored Troops.

Food, our second theme, emphasizes the provisioning of the army. The US Army's Commissary General depended on a network of shippers and suppliers that stretched all the way to the frontier farms of the region. Midwest millers ground wheat into flour, which was shipped to the front and baked into bread in huge army kitchens. Local bakers turned out hardtack to be packed and shipped in wooden crates. Slaughterhouses butchered Midwestern hogs and beef cattle for salt meat and companies shipped it to the war zone by the barrel. Livestock dealers bought herds of cattle and moved them on the hoof to supply fresh meat to the soldiers.

The third theme considers the region's abundant natural resources and raw materials and their roles in securing victory for the Union. Indiana's coal production more than tripled to meet northern industry's need for fuel. The demand for bullets encouraged expanded lead mining in Iowa, Illinois, and Wisconsin. Michigan produced salt, copper, oil, natural gas, and iron ore to be made into cannons, steam engines, railroad tracks, and more. The expansive forests of Minnesota, Michigan, and Wisconsin were harvested and converted into towns, supply depots, plank roads, crates, wagons, cannon carriages, and fuel. Major cities on the Great Lakes such as Chicago, Detroit, and Milwaukee became transportation hubs for railroads and shipping.

Another key element to the Midwest in the Civil War program is *Seeing the Elephant*. Teachers commented that the film helps students better visualize battle and the soldier experience while providing a clearer view of the Civil War era. Evaluations show the movie successfully helps students emotionally connect with how the war affected these local men and their families back home, again reinforcing that Midwestern connection.

After their staff- and docent-led portion of Midwest in the Civil War, we give students prepared questions to answer. Students work in small groups, explore the exhibit on their own, interpret artifacts, and draw conclusions about the questions posed. They reunite with their class to report on their findings and opinions. This approach allows us to concentrate on teaching content while putting students in control of their learning experience and thus build critical thinking skills.

Other school programs use individual narratives to reinforce the importance of the Upper Midwest to the war effort. Two examples are Major James Pond of the 3rd Wisconsin Cavalry and Caroline Quarlls of Sandwich, Ontario, Canada. The Pond family moved to Illinois from upstate New York when James was a boy because his father was seeking available land and economic opportunity. The family moved to Wisconsin and as James grew up, he became active in printing and journalism. During the war, he served with the 3rd Wisconsin Cavalry and was awarded the Medal of Honor for his actions at Baxter Springs, Kansas. In discussing Pond's story, we ask students to reflect on their own histories of moving. This allows us to lead discussion about immigration to the Upper Midwest before the Civil War, the reasons why people moved to the region, and connects these tales to students' own experiences.

In 1842, Caroline Quarlls became the first documented fugitive slave conducted through the Wisconsin network to freedom. Quarlls was a sixteen-year-old slave living in St. Louis before she made her escape. Even more astounding is that she left a detailed written record of her journey and her life afterward in Canada. These primary sources serve as a starting point for the discussion of Midwestern attitudes towards slavery, abolition, and emancipation and attach a local face to the story of the enslavement of African Americans.

Education staff at the Civil War Museum have also partnered with local volunteers, reenactors, as well as teachers from two local middle schools to present "Field Day." This exposes students to a variety of Civil War topics using outdoor demonstrations, exhibits, and the museum's film. Six hundred middle school students and teachers are divided into eight equal-sized groups to experience the program and allow for more small group learning with the eight to ten reenactor stations each visits for ten minutes. When ten minutes has passed, an audio prompt—the firing of a cannon—tells the students to move onto their next station. At each station, reenactors present interpretations on medical care and surgery, artillery firing, infantry tactics, the Signal Corps, nursing, and the 29th United States Colored Troops.

Living History

At many historic sites and to a lesser extent, museums, costumed interpreters are a part of the regular paid staff. Whether interpreting via first or third person, they very easily and effectively bring people of the past to life for visitors. Unfortunately, most museums cannot afford to pay costumed interpreters, but there is another way.

Interpreting the Civil War in any part of the country can be enhanced through the use of well-trained volunteer reenactors. Many museum professionals view reenactors as novices that should not be utilized. Civil War reenactors can be an asset when they are properly trained by staff just as any other volunteer would be trained in their subject matter and its appropriate delivery. Most of the reenactors that we utilize on a regular basis represent companies from Illinois and Wisconsin. Bringing Midwestern soldiers to life solidifies the local history connection. We have found it is a powerful form of interpretation. For guests, seeing what a soldier ate; how he marched, loaded, and fired rifles and artillery; and/or how medical procedures were handled leaves a lasting impression that extends beyond the museum visit.

Reenactors are docents. They should be held accountable just like any other volunteer. Their job is to impart accurate information to the public in an engaging manner. As such they are held to the same standards as any other volunteer. A new docent is less prepared in terms of subject matter and appropriate presentation technique than a good reeanactor. A useful reenactor is one who understands the museum's objectives, enjoys teaching, and has an outgoing personality. A reenactor who looks the part but knows little history is of little use to the museum and should be gently released. Some of our best reenactors are teachers by profession. They travel to the museum at their own expense, utilize their own gear and offer numerous, engaging educational opportunities. Handled well, it can be a win/win for all.

Both the museum and reanactors must start with a mutual respect for each other. It is no different from working with any other volunteer who is accepted into the system. Will there be complications? Of course, but no more than what you experience with other volunteers.

Conclusion

At first glance, the idea of building a Civil War museum on the western shore of Lake Michigan seems, at best, ill advised. Nationally, the Civil War is perceived as an Eastern and Southern event that had little to do with the Midwest. We knew that going in but we had a little known story to tell. We did not want to duplicate what already existed and we needed to appeal to a wide audience.

Utilizing multiple approaches to impart information that the Midwestern region was a major part of the war was essential. If we were to be successful, we needed to appeal to a broad demographic, not just to those with a passion for military history. The war is perceived by the public as a story about men fighting and little else. In reality, like any war, the Civil War involved men, women, children, people of differing economic status as well as people of different ethnic and national backgrounds. Humanizing those sepia-toned figures and telling their story was central.

Tackling these issues from different angles was exhilarating, but choosing from the endless number of Midwestern Civil War stories was difficult. In order to create a memorable visit and increase our visitors' appreciation of the sacrifices of our ancestors, we decided on presenting Midwestern stories set in a national context. These are rich and interesting stories on a scale that visitors relate to easily and enable them to better develop empathy. Doing this in an immersive environment with a myriad of different methods of information delivery appeals to multiple learning styles. This approach makes our visitor experience and the information presented memorable.

By definition, history is about people. When we are at our best, museums are the storytellers that help our visitors empathize with people of the past. The personal stories of men, women, and children make the museum and the history contained within more accessible and meaningful to a wider audience. Maintaining the humanity in history is important in not only connecting with our public—it is important in telling a military history that visitors can relate to easily.

A Civil War museum in the Midwest? Yes, it is not only possible but it can be successful, annually drawing over 75,000 visitors. At every step within the museum we illustrate the important place the Upper Midwest and its people had in the war and we do it in a multitude of ways that leave a lasting impression on the visitor. At the end of "The Fiery Trial," our visitors leave with a better sense of their region's place in the larger conflict, the sacrifices made by people just like them, and the war's continuing impact on our lives.

CHAPTER 4

Civil War Public History for the Next Generation

James Percoco

THE ANCIENT ROMANS HAD a phrase, "genius loci," referring to the protective spirit of a place. During the course of my thirty-two years I leveraged that ancient admonition in my history classes at West Springfield High School in Fairfax, Virginia, particularly for twenty-two of those years in my public history course called Applied History. Students enrolled in this senior elective were with me in a traditional classroom setting for the first semester, studying a variety of topics, rooted in primary sources and looking in particular at the role of memory in the construction of history. During the second semester these same students, then with early release time, worked at local historic sites and museums in Northern Virginia and Washington, DC. The Smithsonian's National Museum of American History, Ford's Theatre, George Washington's home and estate, Mount Vernon, the Alexandria Black History Museum and the Fairfax Museum were just a few of the places where my students contributed one hundred hours from January through June to assisting staff at these sites either working as docents, in some cases in costume, working in collections management, public programming, or developing learning materials for younger students.

Historic sites and museums are natural partners for schools. Working together schools and public history institutions can foster a larger sense of community, shared experiences, and provide space for not only place-based learning but service learning endeavors as well. I take great pride in the fact that many of my students went to work for the National Park Service, mostly in the arena of interpretation. Growing up in Massachusetts on the fringes of Minute Man National Historical Park, my impression of history was shaped tremendously by the National Park Service. In some ways as a teacher I have been able to give back to the National Park Service, in what has been a more than five-decade love affair.

Applying an Applied History Approach

Like politics, all history is at its deepest level local. It matters not where you work to be able to connect your programs to both public and private schools. As a public historian or museum education specialist you might need to take the first step to launch a working relationship with your local schools. A simple phone call to local museums and historic sites is all that it takes for you to get the ball rolling for you and your students. With the push to improve student learning and outcomes in history and more and more schools across the country requiring for graduation some component of service learning, the time is ripe for museum or historic site staff everywhere to join the bandwagon.

The kind of student learning that takes place at museums and historic sites is the ultimate hands-on experience. During the course of my teaching applied history I had the deep satisfaction of watching my students immerse themselves in "the stuff" of history, particularly those who worked in collections management positions. One of my students working at the Newseum was given the project of cataloging all the artifacts in famed World War II correspondent Edward R. Murrow's World War II trunk. Another student working in the political history division of the National Museum of American History was there on the day that pointers used by H. Ross Perot in a 1992 television appearance arrived at the museum. Several students participated in the recovery of the remains of Union soldiers buried in Centerville, Virginia, on the site of where a McDonald's was being built, while others working at historic Congressional Cemetery helped the staff there develop, by using old newspaper accounts, fuller stories of those buried in the cemetery, ranging from people who were somehow connected with the Lincoln assassination, the Civil War, or the era of bootlegging and Prohibition.

I was always amazed, astounded, and gratified by the stories of my students who were able to see and feel a tangible connection to the past. Visiting these students and sharing in their enthusiasm made me proud of them and yearn for more ways to connect my students with the power of place and objects as we collectively studied history. One of my biggest success stories as a teacher is with the young woman who is now the Supervisory Park Ranger at Wright Brothers National Memorial on the Outer Banks of North Carolina. Jin worked as an intern at Arlington House. She transitioned to a part-time ranger while attending George Mason University in Fairfax, Virginia. Because she worked hard she was able to work summers as a seasonal ranger at Hawaii Volcano's National Monument and at Yosemite National Park. Once she graduated from George Mason University she immediately became a full-time ranger. Jin once told me that her experience in applied history shaped the trajectory of her life. After first working at Great Falls National Park in Virginia she moved onto Zion National Park. It all came back full circle for me when I was contacted by the National Park Service human resources staff to discuss her application for the job she now holds at Wright Brothers National Memorial.

My regular US history classes were also able to get in on the action as I was able to dispatch them to museums on what I term *independent study trips*. In this scenario I scoped out various museum exhibitions, like the one on the American Presidency at the Smithsonian's National Museum of American History, the National Portrait Gallery's exhibition on the Age of Theodore Roosevelt, and the National Archives Exhibit "Our Documents." In all of these cases I contacted museum staff and pre-visited the museum myself to see what kinds of activities I could immerse my students in during the visit. Thus many of them trundled off to these various museums with clipboards and activity sheets in hand that I used for assessment purposes. I also worked hard to align these visits with the Standards of Learning for Virginia so that there was a component of their learning connected to specific content required for the mandated year-end testing. For example, in the Smithsonian's exhibit on the American Presidency one of the sections of the exhibit looked at the role of the president as a communicator and one of the objects on display was a microphone used by President Franklin Delano Roosevelt to deliver any number of fireside chats. The exhibit also included audio recordings of Roosevelt's fireside chats. Fireside chats were something that the Virginia Standards of Learning addressed, thus rather than being told about them in a lecture, students could "see" and "hear" at the same time this crucial element of Roosevelt's legacy as president. For the National Portrait Gallery's exhibit on President Theodore Roosevelt there was a significant examination, through objects, photographs, and primary sources related to the building of the Panama Canal. Here, too, I was able to segue back to the Virginia Standards of Learning. In teaching and presenting material in such a way teachers end up "showing" students history, not "telling" them history. It is a great way to make connections that are difficult to make inside the four walls of a classroom.

Civil War–related sites are unique from other historic sites in that they remain places of contested national memory. In some ways, we are still fighting the Civil War long after Ulysses S. Grant and Robert E. Lee signed capitulation documents at Appomattox Court House, Virginia, also a unit in the National Park Service. Another draw to working with Civil War sites is their immense popularity with the public. Students who work at our national battlefields and military parks see a large cross section of our population that permits them to engage a broader public.

It is also at these sites of contested memory that students, like park staff, have to wrestle with issues that pervade our popular culture when it comes to the Civil War. Because issues are so contentious at these sites students can't escape being drawn into the national conversation. It is important for young people to see how that is worked out both behind the scenes and in policy decisions, which can reflect how a place or object at that place is interpreted.

The Nuts and Bolts of Constructing a New Approach to Teaching and Learning

Let me address the nuts and bolts of how to pull this off. I worked closely with several Civil War sites in the National Park Service when I taught applied history at West Springfield High School. In two of the cases I contacted the parks directly, Ford's Theatre National Historic Site and Manassas National Battlefield. Through my work there I was contacted by staff at Arlington House National Historic Site: The National Memorial to Robert E. Lee to see if they could become part of the program. I immediately brought them into the fold. I also had students work at Historic Blenheim, a former plantation home in Fairfax City, Virginia. During the Civil War as Union forces occupied Fairfax many took up quarters in Blenheim. Some of these soldiers left graffiti writing on the walls in the interior of the house, thus locally it is called the "Graffiti House."

One of the differences in having students work at smaller sites than Park Service units is that they tend to run extensive hands-on weekend programs all year long. For example, at Blenheim they host an annual Civil War Days. Staff members at Blenheim were able to use students to not only help prep for the two-day affair, but also to man the variety of booths that were part of the official events. Students who work at National Park Sites get a lesson in "government bureaucracy" as well as learn the kinds of skills in collections management and curatorial work. At smaller sites, there is much more of a grass roots experience for students who get to really connect local history to the larger national narrative.

I suggest that you build contacts with local schools. You will need to do some reconnaissance. Find the name of a specific teacher to whom you might wish to contact. If you send a letter to the principal, it will take some time to filter down to the teachers, so reach out to someone who you think might be willing to jump-start the program with you. Frame your pitch as an opportunity not only for place-based learning, but for service learning as well. Many school districts in their central offices have social studies specialists, who can help to locate potential teacher participants. Be enthusiastic in your approach. Don't get frustrated if someone at the administrative level demurs. In your pitch demonstrate how students working at your site will have a direct connection to the C3 Framework, focusing on college, career, and civic life. Consider, as Arlington House did, offering students summer employment as seasonal rangers when their internships are completed. Thirty-six of my students ended up wearing the uniform and badge of the National Park Service, including the chief of interpretation at Wright Brothers National Memorial in North Carolina.

One thing to consider is whether or not students will have transportation to your site. Living in the suburbs of Washington, DC, with its network of roads made it easier for students with driver licenses to get to and from their respective sites. Given that many Civil War battlefields are in rural areas this factor needs to be taken into consideration. Provide students opportunities to work on weekends, which is when most of mine completed their work responsibilities.

It generally takes a month or so for students to get acclimated to the site. Most of my students spent the first month going over the site's interpretative plan. Those students who wanted to work directly with the public giving program talks were given free rein to develop their own interpretation of the site relating stories that could best connect them with their audience. This was most evident with students that worked at Ford's Theatre and at Arlington House, where they gave presentations in period costume. Other students opted to work in collections management and engaged in cataloging projects or developing programs for the site that complied with the Americans with Disabilities Act. In one case a student developed programs for the blind that incorporated braille into the site's interpretive plan.

What was interesting to observe as their teacher was how by working at these sites students came to develop their own understanding of how the Civil War fits into the national narrative. Their interpretations, particularly those that were giving talks, addressed the National Park Service's efforts to interpret the Civil War from a broader and more diverse platform. At Arlington House, much of the interpretation addressed the lives of the enslaved population at Lee's home and then the lives of those who lived on the property as freedmen after the war. In this way history was interpreted from "the bottom up" as opposed to from the "great man" premise that has long been a staple at Civil War sites. My students worked hard with park staff to recover the lost voices of the past.

The specific projects on which my students worked with museum and park staff were wide ranging. In the six months that students spent at the site some students were given multiple projects depending on what the site needed. For example, at the Graffiti House, where much of the Civil War graffiti was up in the attic, fire codes would not permit visitor access. So, the staff had students working there digitally recording the images for a faux attic exhibit developed for the main gallery. There was even a ribbon-cutting ceremony for the new exhibit in which my students participated. At Ford's Theatre, students researched the lives of some of the principles, who were in the Theatre at the time of Lincoln's assassination and compiled the information they gleaned by researching into the revised master plan for the site.

Another site I worked with, Congressional Cemetery, in Washington, DC, contains the remains of many people who played a role in the Civil War such as Mathew Brady, some of the Lincoln conspirators, and the women who died in the 1862 Arsenal Fire. For fund raising efforts students dug through old obituaries and other archival documents to help develop "Living History" programs for days that were set aside for people to do first-person interpretation at the person's gravesite. Burgeoning local actors were given the biographical information researched by the students to help them better flesh out their performance for visitors.

If your site like Antietam National Battlefield has memorial illumination programs, reach out to local schools to get them involved. For many years, my students and I participated in the Antietam National Battlefield Memorial Illumination as volunteers setting up luminaries in the fields of the Mumma Farm. This always proved to be a winning event for my students, as they believed that they were genuinely giving back to those who lost their lives on that fateful September 17, 1862. For many the pay-off was that they were part of a larger whole, particularly during the evening's drive through the park to see the more than 23,100 luminaries lit. The sheer volume of flickering candles makes the number of casualties a stark reality as opposed to a cold statistic. Antietam's program has launched similar programs at Civil War sites across the country at places like Gettysburg and Andersonville. Even if you are a public historian working at a state or local park as opposed to a national park consider creating your own luminary event. They are powerful and evocative and get students to think about commemoration and memorialization well beyond the static bronze or stone monument. Again, reach out to schools in your community and offer it as a way for students from your local schools to participate in similar service-learning projects. One of my former favorite students who is now a public historian with the National Trust for Historic Preservation wrote her college essay based on her experience at Antietam. In her application essay, Priya was able to talk intelligently as a high school senior about public history and why it is important. "I'll never forget the Memorial Illumination," she wrote in her reflective journal entry. "It was so overpowering to see all those candles lit and even more overpowering to know that I had been able to transcend time by helping to place and then light hundreds of them."

To ensure a successful program whether it is an internship experience project or participation in a commemorative event, site staff need to be enthusiastic and passionate, not only about their park, site, or museum, but also about working with young people. Your work with students will not achieve anything if you regulate them to licking stamps and stuffing envelopes. You need to get to know the students you are working with on a personal level. Treat them as equals or co-partners not as "gophers." Let the students guide you with their particular interests. Lay out for them different options which might best tailor to their interests and learning style or ask them what they are interested in and see if you can craft something that is needed for your site to meet the needs of the students.

I also suggest that you interview prospective interns. During the twenty-two years that I taught applied history I did have some unmotivated students, but I always worked with those students and staff to find the right fit. Many of my students were also in the performing arts program at school. When Arlington House had a program in 2010 to commemorate the 150th anniversary of the election of 1860 many students flocked to be able to be players of roles wearing costumes. It was a lot of fun for them as they re-created encounters between Lincoln enthusiasts, as Wide Awakes bearing torches, and supporters of Stephen A. Douglas and other politicians on the 1860 slate. Arlington House's staff helped students write scripts and taught them to understand history without the use of a textbook, mostly relying on primary material related to 1860 newspaper editorials or personal correspondence of the slate of candidates. Before the event there was a great deal of give and take between site staff and historians, myself, and my students.

Conclusion

One of my former teaching colleagues was fond of saying that "history is a contact sport." He was spot on, particularly when students encounter history by working in a hands-on project in an atmosphere where professionalism and collegiality play such an important role. Places like Gettysburg, Vicksburg, Shiloh, and Antietam provide the fields on which hands-on history indeed becomes a contact sport in more ways than one. Working at such sites in a variety of capacities forces students to contend with the facts the site presents as either "history" or "memory." No matter what the students come up with as an answer to some of our toughest national questions in the public discourse it will prove to be a memorable and potentially life changing experience, and both the students and the sites at which they find themselves plying their new trade will be equally better for it.

CHAPTER 5

New Wine in Old Bottles

Using Historical Markers to Reshape Public Memory of the Civil War

W. Todd Groce

IN APRIL 2014 THE *Wall Street Journal* published an article that pronounced the Civil War sesquicentennial a failure. The profits anticipated at the beginning of the anniversary never materialized due to the downturn in the economy and a general lack of interest in celebrating the war. Unlike the centennial, the sesquicentennial just didn't measure up. Crowds did not turn out for reenactments and attendance at national battlefields was way down compared to 50 years earlier.[1]

But if the *WSJ* was paying attention, it would have noticed that financial profit was not the goal of those who organized the Civil War sesquicentennial. The public history institutions that took part in the commemoration sought something more important and lasting—to change perceptions about the war and its relevance to modern Americans. The thrust of the Civil War 150 was to bring a new understanding based on modern scholarship. We aimed for education, not celebration.[2]

Because there was no federal commission as there had been during the centennial, organizers of the sesquicentennial were concerned that there would never be a national conversation about the war's deeper meaning. In particular, they feared that discussions about race and slavery—topics that were central to the conflict but impossible to talk about fifty years earlier in the early 1960s—would be lost in a sea of reenactments, battlefield tours, and other celebratory activities sponsored by those who wanted to glorify the war and its heroism and those who simply wanted to cash in on it.

The lack of national direction forced planning down to the state and local level where, not surprisingly, the quality and quantity of activities was uneven at best. Under intense pressure to meet basic services at a time of shrinking revenue, most states had little money to fund activities. This left direction of the commemoration to the private sector—and shaped the nature of the commemoration in ways that otherwise might not have been possible.

Challenging the Traditional Narrative

A leader in Georgia's sesquicentennial commemoration was the Georgia Historical Society (GHS), the independent, statewide research and educational institution responsible for collecting and teaching Georgia history. Through a private-public partnership, since 1998 GHS has installed and maintained the state's historical markers, and we saw the Civil War 150 as an opportunity to use the program to generate a statewide conversation about the war and its legacy in the twenty-first century. Historical markers are a unique way to tell new stories about marginalized people and long-ignored events and to bring to the general public the scholarship of credentialed, professional historians that often contradicts folklore and myths. GHS already had extensive experience in creating historical markers about difficult and controversial subjects in the state's history—topics like lynching, civil rights protests, racially motivated murders, and slavery—and had seen how effective such marker topics were in generating meaningful discussion about how the past influences the present and shapes the future. So it was only natural that GHS decided to create a project using historical markers to tell stories about the Civil War that would offer a clearer understanding of the conflict, its causes, and legacy, and that would challenge popular notions about the war based on the hazy nostalgia of the Lost Cause.[3]

Thus the goal of the Civil War 150 Historical Marker Project was to promote tourism while at the same time helping Georgians and visitors alike to see the war in new and different ways. To do this we would use the oldest (and some would argue most outmoded) form of public history—historical markers—and couple it with modern technology. By telling new stories—or in some cases, telling old stories in new ways—the project would encourage Georgians to appreciate the multi-faceted and complex nature of the war, and that the history of the event could and should extend far beyond the battlefield, none of which was conveyed in the older centennial period markers put up during the 1950s and 1960s. To employ a well-known biblical metaphor, we were pouring new wine into old bottles—presenting new interpretations on old-style markers—to broaden the story of the Civil War and give it new meaning for the twenty-first century.

In order to get a handle on the task before us, GHS undertook the first-ever official survey of existing Civil War markers in Georgia, most of them erected fifty years earlier in anticipation of the war's centennial. The survey revealed quantitatively what we already knew qualitatively: there were nearly a thousand historical markers in Georgia about the Civil War and nearly all of them (92 percent) were about some military aspect of the conflict. Nearly all were written through the lens of the Lost Cause, a narrative constructed in the late nineteenth century as a way to explain Confederate defeat, glorify Confederate leaders, and to justify the Southern independence movement as a fight for Constitutional liberty rather than an attempt to create a new nation founded upon slavery and white supremacy. Despite half a century of scholarly research that clearly demonstrated slavery's central role as the cause for the war, many Georgians at the beginning of the twenty-first century continued to accept the Lost Cause narrative and to romanticize and glorify the Confederacy while minimizing slavery's role in the conflict. Thus, the challenge as the sesquicentennial began was how to make the scholarly research that countered the Lost Cause narrative accessible to a wide audience and thereby demonstrate the war's relevance to all Americans.[4]

To that end, over the course of the sesquicentennial, GHS and its partners—the Georgia Department of Economic Development, Georgia Department of Labor, and the Georgia Battlefields Association—erected twenty new historical markers across the state. These markers were on topics that had been overlooked in the 1950s and 1960s and that incorporated the findings of Civil War scholars over the last generation, all of which challenged the traditional narrative of a monolithic white South committed to the Confederacy. They explored slavery's role as the cause of the conflict, Unionism and dissent, labor unrest at factories, women and food riots, African Americans in combat and slave uprisings, and anti-Confederate activity among Georgia's white population. They challenged the myth of the black Confederate and acknowledged the desire to preserve slavery as the cause of secession. They demonstrated that Georgians had rebelled openly against the Confederacy and that many had fought in arms to oppose it.

In order to select the proper topics for the new markers, GHS assembled a team of historians, including on-staff experts, to advise us in the process. The outside consultants who generously volunteered their time and expertise were faculty from the University of Georgia, Valdosta State University, and the University of West Georgia, as well as specialists from the Atlanta History Center and one independent scholar. After choosing the themes for the new markers—slavery, Unionism, anti-Confederate resistance, the homefront, labor, and the role of women and African Americans—we identified specific people and events, the stories of which could be used as vehicles to illustrate one of the larger themes. Geographic distribution of the markers was also a major consideration as we selected locations across the state where these events occurred. Public safety, of course, also had to be taken into account. We had to make sure that the new markers were placed in locations easily and safely accessed by visitors, whether in automobiles or on foot. This stood in stark contrast to some of the older centennial period markers, one of which was discovered in the middle of an interstate cloverleaf!

The most challenging aspect of creating the new markers was writing the marker text. The markers must not only describe the event but also place it in an interpretive framework while also conveying the meaning and relevancy to the reader. Each must pass what we call the "so what?" test. The reader should never have to wonder why the event described on the marker is important and has meaning. This was a tall order when working with a limit of approximately 130 words. Not surprisingly, each marker went through multiple drafts as we carefully weighed each word. Unlike the earlier markers, which assumed that the reader had some knowledge of the war and its history, each new marker would begin by explaining that the event occurred during the American Civil War and would be free of the military abbreviations and jargon so common in the older markers, such as using "AC" for army corps. For ease of maintenance as well as clarity, we would refrain from using the small, full-color US and Confederate flags liberally employed in the older markers to identify military units, keeping any description of battles and maneuvers clear and precise. Given the widespread negative reaction against the Rebel flag in wake of the 2015 Charleston shooting of African Americans by a white supremacist, this decision proved the right one in more than one way.

Also, in keeping with modern interpretation, we made a decision to drop the use of the terms *Union* and *Union Army*, opting instead for *United States* and *United States Army*. Following the lead of several renowned historians, such as Gary Gallagher and Gregory Downs, we stopped using the language of the Lost Cause and of the Reconciliation and referred to the armed forces of the United States as they had been during the war itself. Doing so was not only in keeping with original, wartime terminology (one will search in vain for any reference in official wartime documents to the "Union Army"), but it also made clear that the United States did not disappear during the years from 1861 to 1865 as the states divided into something called "the Union" and the Confederacy. Adopting war-time terminology ran counter to the traditional Lost Cause narrative. It allowed us to convey a deeper, more accurate understanding of the conflict shared by both sides during the 1860s— that secessionists were waging war against the government of the United States in order to gain their independence and establish a slaveholders' republic.[5]

None of this would matter, however, if people could not find the markers. A key part of the project was the creation and launch of a micro website and free smart-phone app that would use Google Maps as a way to locate all Civil War markers, existing and new, allowing students, tourists, and history enthusiasts to develop their own custom-designed driving tours based on historical markers. At the time (2009) this innovative, one-of-a-kind, state-of-the art website and app placed Georgia at the forefront of technology-based resources for developing heritage tourism. The website and app also allowed us to promote the project as a way to link historic sites across the state through historical markers. For instance, as tourists followed the route of the March to the Sea, they would pass through towns like Madison, Milledgeville, and Savannah. The website suggested historic sites to visit, places to eat, and other activities to enjoy.

The statewide survey of existing markers also provided data necessary for repairing and replacing damaged and missing markers and global positioning for the creation of technology that would facilitate discovery of the markers and promote tourism in the communities where they were located. Of the 919 markers surveyed, approximately 15 percent were in need of some type of maintenance, usually cleaning or repainting, or total replacement. Realizing that this type of work could potentially consume the entire budget, GHS replaced only seven missing markers, all related to the March to the Sea, making it possible once again for tourists to trace the route of Sherman's army from Atlanta to Savannah using historical markers as guide posts.

Once we were ready to begin installation of the new markers, GHS hired a consultant to help us create a "Story Telling Campaign." The erection of a new marker would be accompanied by a well-publicized dedication ceremony that involved local political and civic leaders. Although the Georgia Historical Society is a statewide public history institution, it

Figure 5.1. Former UN ambassador and civil rights icon Andrew Young with the author at the dedication of the "African American Soldiers in Combat" historical marker in Dalton, Georgia, October 2, 2010. Photo by Matt Hamilton. Courtesy of the *Dalton Daily Citizen*.

is headquartered in Savannah, and we did not want to appear to be dropping into a community, erecting a marker about a potentially controversial subject such as a slave uprising, and then leaving again, all without the support and cooperation of local community leaders. We thus worked hard to establish those connections in each location where we erected a new marker, as well as to generate publicity about the event itself. At the public event dedicating the marker, a historian, preferably a scholar who had written on the marker topic, would deliver a brief address about the history of the event and its larger meaning before the marker was unveiled and added to the website and app. If the marker being dedicated dealt with the role of African Americans in the war, as many of them did, then the ceremony also included remarks by a prominent African American leader in the state, such as Labor Commissioner Michael Thurmond and former Atlanta Mayor and UN Ambassador Andrew Young.

In order for the project to have the greatest impact on both tourism and education GHS decided not to wait on specific anniversary events in order to erect markers. Instead we moved ahead and got as many of them in the ground as possible. We also launched the website and app so that they, too, were operational well ahead of the sesquicentennial start date in the spring of 2011. Specific marker topics and locations included: African American US soldiers in combat near Dalton; General David Hunter's emancipation proclamation that was issued on Tybee Island a year before President Lincoln's; a wartime industrial explosion at a gunpowder factory in Augusta; an attempted slave revolt in the south Georgia town of Quitman; a women's bread riot in Columbus; the role of pro-secession women in funding the construction of a Confederate ironclad in Savannah; the rejected proposal by General Patrick Cleburne to enlist slaves in the Confederate army located at the original Confederate headquarters building in Dalton; Georgia's secession convention in Milledgeville; a massacre of US sympathizers by Confederate guerillas near McCaysville; the enlistment of Georgians in the US forces in the mountains of north Georgia; the March to the Sea at its beginning and ending points in Atlanta and Savannah; the drowning at Ebenezer Creek near Springfield of hundreds of freed slaves who were following Sherman's army during the March; and the subsequent Special Field Order Number 15, the so-called "Forty Acres and a Mule" order issued by the federal government in Savannah.[6]

GHS also provided context for many of the older markers. For instance, there are hundreds of centennial-era markers scattered throughout the Atlanta area describing in minute detail the military battles and maneuvering that led to the fall of the city in September 1864. But there was no one marker that placed all of the fighting and campaigning in proper context. To that end, a marker titled "The Battles for Atlanta" was installed on the grounds of the Carter Center that explained the significance of the city in 1864, why the armies were contending for it, the five major engagements that were fought around the city, and why its capture by US forces matters still today—because it ensured the re-election of Abraham Lincoln as president of the United States and with that the doom of the Confederacy. For those using the website and app, this marker served as the starting point for any driving tour of the city.

Publicly addressing slavery as the cause of the war was a prime objective of the project. Slavery's role in triggering secession had not been acknowledged in the centennial-era markers, reflecting the more traditional Lost Cause interpretation that slavery was only the pretext, not the cause, of the war. In the intervening decades since the end of the centennial, this "secession without slavery" interpretation had been completely overturned by modern scholarship and the new markers needed to reflect that change. Accordingly, on January 19, 2011, the 150th anniversary of the passage of the Georgia Ordinance of Secession, GHS dedicated in front of the Civil War capitol at Milledgeville a marker about the secession convention, the first ever to cover exclusively that event. The marker explained that secession in Georgia began as a response to the election of Abraham Lincoln and the belief that his Republican Party was "anti-slavery in its mission and its purpose," to quote the Secession Ordinance's Declaration of Causes.[7]

Another objective of the project was to address the modern-day myth about the widespread enlistment of blacks in the Confederate army. Dalton was the location of the only battle in which African American soldiers fought in Georgia and a marker telling that story was installed at the site of the fort they defended. After being captured, the enlisted men of the 44th United States Colored Troops were sent back into slavery in accordance with Confederate policy, countering the idea that there existed substantial Confederate support for black soldiers. The dedication in October 2010 featured a keynote address by former UN ambassador and Atlanta mayor Andrew Young and was attended by a diverse audience of nearly five hundred people. Another marker erected in Dalton related the story of the aborted proposal by Confederate General Patrick Cleburne in early 1864 to arm and free slaves to fight in the Confederate army. The proposal was rejected by both the Rebel high command and the government as "hideous" and contrary to the reasons why the slave-holding states had seceded in the first place. This marker demonstrated that there was no enlistment of black Confederate soldiers, nor any widespread support among Confederate civilians, soldiers, officers, or government officials to do so, all myths that continue to be espoused widely on the Internet.

Other markers in the project told the largely unknown story of Georgians who fought against the Confederacy. A marker dedicated in the town of Blue Ridge in October 2012 related the tale of William Clayton Fain, one of a handful of delegates who refused to sign the Georgia Ordinance of Secession and returned to his mountain home to oppose the Confederacy until killed by Confederate guerillas. At the dedication ceremony David Ralston, Speaker of the Georgia House of Representatives and a resident of Blue Ridge, delivered the keynote address, noting the strong Unionism of many north Georgians, including some of his own ancestors. Another marker erected in nearby McCaysville related the story of Georgia Unionists who were massacred by Confederate guerillas as they attempted to reach Tennessee and enlist in the US Army. Approximately five thousand Georgians served with US forces against the Confederacy, and a marker in Dawsonville told the story about the First Georgia Infantry (US), which was primarily raised in that area.

GHS also decided it was time to highlight Georgia's pro-Union leaders who had served on the national stage, bringing to them the same level of attention that had been lavished in the past on Confederates James Longstreet, Joe Wheeler, and John B. Gordon. In December 2012, retired US Army General Montgomery Meigs spoke at the dedication of the historical marker at the Augusta birth site of his ancestor and namesake, Montgomery Meigs, who served as quartermaster general of the US Army during the Civil War and created America's premier national cemetery in Arlington, Virginia. Another marker was erected in Savannah at the birthplace of US General John C. Fremont, the famous "Pathfinder of the West." Meigs and Fremont were the only native Georgians who served as general officers in the US Army during the war and their stories had never been told anywhere in the country through a historical marker. Everyone did not appreciate this correction. Shortly after the dedication of the Montgomery Meigs marker, we received a letter complaining about our decision to "honor" a man who was a "traitor" to his native state and region. Meigs would no doubt have replied to this charge of treason against the South as he did during the war by stating that throughout his life he had been loyal to the only government he had ever sworn fealty to: the United States of America.[8]

Generating Conversation and Controversy

But it was the marker about "The Burning and Destruction of Atlanta" and those about "The March to the Sea" that best illustrate how the program challenged the standard narrative and engaged the public in reinterpreting the past. Surprisingly, there had never been a marker about the burning of Atlanta, so central to the final outcome of the Civil War, nor had one ever been proposed. When GHS announced plans to install one at the site where the destruction began along present-day Martin Luther King Jr. Drive, we unexpectedly encountered opposition from the Atlanta chapter of the National Association for the Advancement of Colored People (NAACP). For many Americans the Civil War is still equated with glorification of the Confederacy. For over a century, the memory of the war, the suffering of white Southerners, and the exploits of Confederate heroes, was used as a tool for justifying Jim Crow and white supremacy. Many people mistakenly assumed that this new proposed marker would continue that same tradition, and the NAACP argued that such a marker would be an insult to the memory of the martyred civil rights leader. For many others, white and black, influenced by the new scholarship, the war is equated with African American liberation. They understood that a marker at that location about an event that signaled the end of the war and the destruction of the Confederacy (and hence slavery) was eminently appropriate and in keeping with Dr. King's legacy. After consulting with African American leaders in the city and on the GHS Board, we decided to leave the marker in its original location.

The marker was dedicated on April 11, 2011, one day shy of the 150th anniversary of the firing on Fort Sumter. Earlier that day, I appeared on the popular television news program "Good Morning Atlanta" along with the head of the Atlanta NAACP to debate the merits and location of the marker. At the dedication ceremony, former state Labor Commissioner Michael Thurmond, historian Hermina Glass Avery, and Atlanta city councilman Michael Julian Bond, all African Americans, spoke passionately about the appropriateness of the marker's placement. For weeks the debate went on in the Atlanta media. Former US congressman and civil rights leader Julian Bond weighed in with an eloquently composed editorial in the *Atlanta Journal-Constitution* urging African Americans to stop allowing the losers to define the war and instead to begin emphasizing the conflict's positive results—the preservation of the United States and the destruction of slavery.[9]

Three and a half years later, in November and December 2014, the Civil War 150 Historical Marker Project was completed with the installation of two new historical markers on William T. Sherman's March to the Sea. Dedicated on the 150th anniversary of the beginning and ending of the so-called Savannah Campaign, these markers—one in Atlanta where the march began and one in Savannah where it ended—provided an interpretive overview previously lacking for the approximately fifty existing markers installed decades earlier by the State of Georgia along the route of the march. Based on modern scholarship, which exploded Lost Cause mythology about the purpose and results of the campaign, these markers not surprisingly contradict legends and family lore about the extent and nature of the destruction.

Unlike any of the previous markers, those about the March to the Sea touched a nerve with some white Georgians. Despite decades of scholarly research demonstrating that Sherman's destruction was primarily limited to foodstuffs, livestock, factories, and railroads, the suggestion that most, if not all, private homes in Georgia were not burned (unlike in South Carolina) triggered an angry reaction from those raised on stories of white Southern victimization. What appeared to upset many people was that we also explained Sherman's March as a military campaign that ultimately hastened an end to the conflict, destroyed slavery, and reunified the nation. This put the March to the Sea in a new light and suggested that perhaps there were positive effects to the event and all its attendant suffering.[10]

Shortly after the first marker was dedicated in Atlanta in November 2014, letters to the editor appeared in newspapers across Georgia denouncing the marker as historical revisionism and "political correctness" run amok. By the time the second marker was installed

Figure 5.2. The March to the Sea historical marker in Savannah. Photo by Brendan Crellin. Courtesy Georgia Historical Society.

in Savannah in early December, GHS had become the target of a letter writing campaign demanding that we either change the marker to reflect traditional interpretations or remove it altogether. Most of these letters invoked Lost Cause language and deplored "politically correct" historical revisionism: "I am making a formal request that this marker be either removed or corrected to be truthful regarding the glorification of the campaign of war crimes committed by General Sherman and his men during the War Between the States," was typical. Their formulaic nature suggested that the writers of these letters had been given a template or a list of points for objection—not only was our interpretation patently false, they charged, it was offensive and hurtful to the feelings of the letter writers, who considered themselves and their ancestors insulted by the marker text.[11]

Realizing that no amount of evidence or scholarship would change the opinion of those whose minds were closed or who were convinced our project was politically motivated, GHS responded only to thoughtful letters from writers seeking more information from scholarly sources, with one exception. In May 2015, former president Jimmy Carter wrote a letter asking that the March to the Sea marker on the grounds of the Carter Center in Atlanta either be moved or re-written to reflect a more traditional Lost Cause interpretation. The marker had been approved the previous year by the Carter Center and had been in the ground for seven months when, for reasons unclear to us, we received this letter from President Carter reversing course. Despite a reply letter from GHS citing the extensive scholarly sources used to compose the marker text, President Carter remained firm in his request. With the blessings of the city of Atlanta, GHS relocated the marker to nearby Freedom

Park, only a few hundred yards away from its original location, and left the text unaltered. As it turned out, the marker probably is more widely read and more accessible in a busy city park, visited by tens of thousands each year, than when it was located on private property.[12]

Only once over the course of the six-year project did someone show up to protest the installation of a marker. At the close of the dedication ceremony for the second March to the Sea marker in Savannah I was accosted by an older Savannah resident, who happened to also be an acquaintance of mine. "Some of us still remember," she declared in a private conversation as guests were leaving the ceremony. Obviously she wasn't alive during the Civil War. But memory of the war is not confined to eye-witnesses. It has been transmitted across time by the cult of the Lost Cause. "My grandmother told me that Sherman burned all the houses to the ground. Are you telling me she was a liar?" I assured her that I was not accusing her grandmother of lying, adding that I was quite sure her grandmother genuinely believed what she had been told as a child during the 1880s about the March to the Sea. But a grandmother's childhood memories, I explained, were not a substitute for scholarly research and rigorous historical analysis. I added that her issue was not with GHS, but with the historical scholarship on the march. The marker did not reflect simply the opinion of GHS, but the overwhelming body of research on the topic. This exchange not only demonstrated the persistence after a century of folklore at odds with the historical scholarship, it also revealed a curious belief among some people that nearness in time bestows a more accurate understanding of an event.

No segment of the population embraced the project more than Georgia's African Americans, whose involvement (the NAACP opposition notwithstanding) was one of the most successful aspects of Georgia's sesquicentennial. African Americans were central to the Civil War; and no war in American history was so central to the story of African Americans. It was crucial for the success of the project that we encourage audiences to understand the war not as simply an event that affected whites, but also blacks. Not only did GHS focus on telling stories about the role that African Americans and slavery played in the conflict and its origins, we encouraged African American participation at every step in the process, from the selection of the marker topics to the dedication ceremonies. Speakers like Georgia Commissioner of Labor Michael Thurmond, the first African American elected to statewide office since Reconstruction, historians Hermina Glass Avery and Charles Elmore, and Ambassador Andrew Young assured participation by all races in the project and demonstrated the relevance of the war to all Georgians.[13]

Securing African American participation sometimes meant tackling difficult subjects that made some people uncomfortable and demonstrated that our attitudes about the past can be just as racially divided as the way we see the present. As a prelude to the sesquicentennial, in 2008 the Georgia Historical Society and the City of Savannah installed a historical marker for the 150th anniversary of "The Weeping Time," the largest slave sale in American history. The Weeping Time was a tragic event that helped propel the nation toward civil war and one that is still a living memory for Savannah's African American community. Over a two-day period in March 1859, McIntosh County planter Pierce Butler sold at auction 436 men, women, and children, breaking up families, many of whom never reunited. The marker is at the site of the sale, an old racetrack, which today is an African American neighborhood on the west side of Savannah. The day of the dedication the *Savannah Morning News* ran a story about the marker and recounted the history of the sale. It was not long before we received a phone call from an angry, older white man, who complained, "I can't believe you're putting up a marker about *that* topic in *that* neighborhood," he exploded. "You're just stirring up trouble. We've talked enough about slavery. Let's just move on."

The dedication ceremony that afternoon was an emotional event. Over three hundred people, white and black, attended the unveiling of the marker. Savannah Mayor Otis Johnson, only the second African American to hold that office in the city's history and a consistent and ardent supporter of the GHS marker program, delivered the keynote. Afterward, several African American men and women expressed gratitude for the marker: "Thank you for finally telling our story," was a universal refrain.

The public reaction to this marker revealed that many Americans have very different and competing notions about what happened in the past and why that past is relevant to the present. If we intend to have a shared vision of where we are going as a nation, then we must have a shared understanding of where we have been, even if we cannot always agree on what our history means. Acknowledging and confronting difficult subjects like slavery, the Civil War, and Jim Crow, the memory of which has traditionally divided our communities along racial lines, can transform these subjects into something that unites our communities. So long as we continue to divide the past along racial lines, then we will continue to divide the present and the future along those lines. But if we can embrace all of our nation's history, whether it is the Civil War or the civil rights movement, and realize that it is a story that belongs to each and every one of us, regardless of our race or religion, or how long our families have been in this country, then perhaps we can begin to heal old wounds and build a better future.[14]

Not surprisingly, while the project received accolades, awards, nationwide media coverage, and support from people who welcomed the opportunity to see the war in a new way, it also generated opposition from individuals and groups influenced by—and who have a stake in maintaining—an older understanding of the war no longer relevant to most modern Americans. Asking twenty-first-century white Georgians to be objective and to set aside preconceived notions about the war, to think anew about a familiar subject, was asking more than some people were capable of doing. But those who objected were the exception, not the rule, and we should not place too much emphasis on them and in the process exaggerate their numbers and influence. The business and political leadership of the state for the most part understood that a new interpretation of our past, one grounded in historical scholarship and that put Georgia on a trajectory toward the future, was long overdue and they applauded our effort to tell the story in an honest and inclusive fashion. As one GHS board member commented, "All we are asking people to do is open their minds to new ideas and to look at the past with a sense of wonderment."[15]

The lesson for public history institutions is that they need not be afraid to present new interpretations so long as that history is grounded in scholarship and research published by credentialed historians. Indeed, we have a responsibility to do so, regardless of whether some individuals or groups object or are "offended" when confronted by interpretations they see as threatening to their "heritage." We cannot allow our institutions to be held back by a few agenda-driven individuals seeking to impose their vision of the past—and hence the future—on the rest of us, especially when their vision is at odds with historical scholarship.

There is an old saying among public relations experts that a little controversy can be a good thing. Our institutions will gain stature and prestige when we demonstrate a willingness to tackle difficult subjects and challenge audiences to think about the past in a new way. Indeed, doing so is at the heart of our mission to help create an educated citizenry and promote a civil society.

Conclusion: A Reshaped Understanding?

So how effective was the Civil War 150 Historical Marker Project? Clearly when the economy tanked in 2008–2009, the anticipated tourism did not materialize. No matter how well designed the project may have been to encourage visitation to the state, there is no way to counter a major downturn in the national economy. Besides, we never developed an effective way to measure the economic impact of the project, forcing us to rely on anecdotal evidence about the affect of marker dedications on a community's economy or of a connection between the project and visitation to historic sites.

As we have seen, limited state funding and the worst economic downturn since the Great Depression meant that education would be the central theme of the sesquicentennial. The private organizations like the Georgia Historical Society that stepped in to fill the gap left by a paucity of state support emphasized education and critical thinking over celebration and placed scholarship above folklore. In fact, one might argue that the reason why the Civil War 150 worked so well in Georgia is that it was de-centralized and largely under private direction. Not-for-profit historical organizations were free to incorporate cutting-edge scholarship in the public programming, to ask hard questions, and discuss controversial topics that were overlooked or considered taboo fifty years ago, and that state and local governments tend to steer clear of in every era.

There is no doubt that the Civil War 150 Marker Project encouraged people to talk about and reexamine their understanding of the war and its legacy. The invitation we extended to the public to stand on new ground and to see the past—and hence the present—in a new way was accepted by many with enthusiasm. Through social media, television interviews, newspaper articles, op-ed postings on the Internet by mainstream media and bloggers, protests by the NAACP and neo-Confederate groups, and spin-off programs such as the one on African Americans and the Civil War organized by the Atlanta Public Library, a statewide conversation was started that contributed to the national discussion about the meaning of the Civil War and how the conflict should be remembered. In the process, it helped set the stage for the ongoing challenges that came at the end of the sesquicentennial to Lost Cause and segregationist-era iconography and its role in modern American society. Moreover, the nature of the project ensures the conversation will not end with the commemoration. Unlike one-off programs such as lectures and seminars, the GHS Civil War markers, like their predecessors from the centennial, will be standing for years to come. They are a legacy that will continue to influence public understanding long after the sesquicentennial is only a memory.

Besides meaningful public conversation about the future of our state and nation, the project produced other important results. It generated extensive African American participation at all levels, something that had been completely lacking during the centennial, making the Civil War a shared national experience relevant to all Americans. Through extensive national media coverage, the project made millions of readers across the country aware of new scholarship and interpretations. The project also cast Georgia in a new light. When in multiple articles the *New York Times* pointed to the GHS markers as evidence of change in our state, it demonstrated to the nation that our people were looking at their past and their future in a new way. At the same time, the project helped Georgians to understand that history is not the same as heritage, and that it is no longer necessary to defend a version of the past inconsistent with the values and aspirations of the twenty-first century.[16]

The ability to achieve all this would not have been possible, however, if Georgians had not been ready for it. As a society we were able during the sesquicentennial to discuss topics like secession and race in a way unimaginable fifty years ago during the centennial. Despite opposition from some people of both races, Georgians overall were receptive to our presentation of recent scholarship and showed that they were willing to question popular understanding of our nation's defining event. The fact that not a single marker was permanently removed or its interpretation altered due to public pressure is testimony to how different the sesquicentennial was from its predecessor, evidence that something had indeed changed in both our state and our nation.[17]

Public conversations, letters to the editor, and local and national media coverage, however, should not be confused with a society-wide change in perspective. As the ongoing debate about Confederate iconography attests, the Lost Cause still has its adherents. It is too soon to measure the full impact of the new markers and other projects in our state and beyond. Besides, education is harder to measure than monetary profit.

But let us not forget that the sesquicentennial began in 2011 with a celebratory Secession Ball in Charleston and ended four years later with the Confederate flag being lowered after half a century at the South Carolina state capitol following the tragic mass shooting in Charleston in 2015. What had been acceptable at the beginning of the 150th anniversary was no longer tolerated as it closed.

In that sense the *Wall Street Journal*'s judgment was premature. The Civil War 150 was a resounding success.

Notes

1. Cameron McWhirter, "For Civil War Buffs, 150-Year Anniversary Has Been Disappointing So Far," *Wall Street Journal*, April 10, 2014.
2. For an excellent overview of the Civil War sesquicentennial's goals and objectives versus those of the centennial, see Rick Beard, "From Civil War to Civil Rights: The Opportunities of the Civil War," *History News* (Summer 2011): 12–15.
3. For more on GHS and its historical marker program, go to www.georgiahistory.com.
4. The best scholarly analysis of the Lost Cause and its continued influence is David Goldfield, *Still Fighting the Civil War: The American South and Southern History* (Baton Rouge: Louisiana State University Press, 2002).

5. For examples of recent works that eschew the use of the terms *Union* and *Union Army* in favor of *United States* and *United States Army*, see Douglas R. Egerton, *Thunder at the Gates: The Black Civil War Regiments That Redeemed America* (New York: Basic Books, 2016); Gary W. Gallagher, *Causes Won, Lost, and Forgotten: How Hollywood and Popular Art Shaped What We Know About the Civil War* (Chapel Hill: University of North Carolina Press, 2008); Gallagher, *The Union War* (Cambridge: Harvard University Press, 2011); Gregory P. Downs, *After Appomattox: Military Occupation and the Ends of War* (Cambridge: Harvard University Press, 2015); and James Lee McDonough, *William Tecumseh Sherman: In the Service of My Country, A Life* (New York: W. W. Norton & Company, 2016).

6. For the full list of Civil War markers installed by GHS for the Civil War 150, go to http://georgiahistory.com/education-outreach/historical-markers/georgia-civil-war-150/.

7. For examples of national coverage of the GHS Georgia secession marker, see Katherine Q. Seelye, "One State Takes a New Look at Causes of the War," *The New York Times*, November 29, 2010; Jeff Jacoby, "Commemorating Secession, with Sorrow and Honesty," *Boston Globe*, January 5, 2011. For the quote from the Georgia Secession Declaration of Causes, see James W. Loewen and Edward H. Sebesta, *The Confederate and Neo-Confederate Reader: The "Great Truth" about the "Lost Cause"* (Jackson: University of Mississippi Press, 2010), 133.

8. For more on Meigs and his loyalty to the United States, see Robert O'Harrow Jr., *The Quartermaster: Montgomery C. Meigs, Lincoln's General, Master Builder of the Union Army* (New York: Simon & Schuster, 2016).

9. Megan Matteucci, "NAACP Objects to MLK Drive Location for Civil War Marker," *Atlanta Journal-Constitution*, April 6, 2011; Ray Henry, "Civil War Marker in Atlanta Stirs Controversy, *Miami Herald*, April 11, 2011; Megan Matteucci, "Plaque May Be Removed From Site," *Atlanta Journal-Constitution*, April 12, 2011; Rick Badie, "King Could Handle the Truth," *Atlanta Journal-Constitution*, April 15, 2011; Bill Torpy, "Controversy Binds Anniversaries," *Atlanta Journal-Constitution*, April 16, 2011; Julian Bond, "Civil War's Winners Worth Celebrating," *Atlanta Journal-Constitution*, April 24, 2011.

10. Two of the best examinations of Sherman, the limits of his "hard hand of war," and the lingering myths surrounding the March to the Sea are John F. Marszalek, *Sherman: A Soldier's Passion for Order* (New York: Free Press, 1993) and Anne Sarah Rubin, *Through the Heart of Dixie: Sherman's March and American Memory* (Chapel Hill: University of North Carolina Press, 2014).

11. For national coverage of the March to the Sea markers, see Alan Blinder, "150 Years Later, Wrestling with a Revised View of Sherman's March," *New York Times*, November 14, 2014; "150 Years Later, Atlanta Challenges Civil War 'Myth,'" *The Take Away* (Public Radio International), November 18, 2014. For examples of letters to the editor in opposition to the markers, see "Sherman's Marker History Inaccurate," *Atlanta Journal-Constitution*, January 1, 2015, and "How Accurate Are Those Historical Markers," *Savannah Morning News*, December 12, 2014.

12. Even after the passage of two and half years since the dedication, outrage over the marker's interpretation continues. See Hank Segars, "Fake History," *Lake Oconee News*, February 23, 2017.

13. For examples of African American participation in the GHS marker dedication ceremonies, see Wayne Hodgin, "Effingham Marker Kicks Off Civil War Project," *Savannah Morning News*, May 26, 2010; Adam Crisp, "Freedom Fighters: Marker Notes Skirmishes by Black Civil War Soldiers," *Chattanooga Times-Free Press*, October 7, 2010; Charles Oliver, "Histor-

ical Marker Can Make a Difference," *Dalton Daily Citizen*, July 15, 2011; Larry Copeland, "Sherman's 'March to the Sea' Still a Sore Subject for Some," *USA Today Special Edition*, July 8, 2013.

14. Since 2008 when GHS brought the story to the nation's attention, the "Weeping Time" has received extensive coverage. See Kristopher Monroe, "The Weeping Time: A Forgotten History of the Largest Slave Auction Ever on American Soil," *The Atlantic*, July 10, 2014. The other African American story brought to national attention by GHS and the Civil War 150 Historical Marker Project was the episode at Ebenezer Creek, where hundreds of fugitive slaves drowned attempting to swim to safety after the US Army they were following took up the pontoon bridges.

15. The GHS Civil War 150 Historical Marker Project received the Georgia Department of Economic Development's 2012 Tourism Championship Partner Award and the American Association for State and Local History's 2011 Leadership in History Award.

16. Katherine Q. Seelye, "One State Takes a New Look at Causes of the War," *New York Times*, November 29, 2010; Alan Blinder, "150 Years Later, Wrestling with a Revised View of Sherman's March," *The New York Times*, November 14, 2014; W. Todd Groce, "Rethinking Sherman's March," *The New York Times*, November 17, 2014.

17. For an examination of the Civil War centennial and American society, see Robert J. Cook, *Troubled Commemoration: The American Civil War Centennial, 1961-1965* (Baton Rouge: Louisiana State University Press, 2007).

CHAPTER 6

From Tokenism to True Partnership

The National Park Service's Shifting Interpretation at the Civil War's Sesquicentennial

John M. Rudy

THE NATIONAL PARK SERVICE'S commemoration of the Civil War sesquicentennial began and ended in Charleston, South Carolina, but not necessarily by design. From Charleston to Charleston, from April 2011 to June 2015, it wound its way across battlefields in Tennessee, Virginia, Mississippi, and Pennsylvania, city streets in Richmond and Washington, DC, fifty-two miles of roadside in Alabama, and the newsfeeds of thousands of Facebook users. Along that journey, that commemoration shifted and changed. The Civil War sesquicentennial we ended was certainly not the one we set out to celebrate.

At the same moment, the craft of interpretation was adapting and changing. The very fabric of how and why we discuss the past with the American people was shifting. In the early 2000s, the National Park Service found itself called by a variety of voices and forces to fundamentally change its core business model. And that shift toward audience-centered experience and critical-issues focused interpretation, very much in its infancy during the four years of Civil War commemoration, still rapidly changes every facet of the work of interpretation.

The Call to Communicate Differently

One of the strongest voices calling for a change in the types of experiences parks offer was the Organization of American Historians (OAH). In 2011, they released *Imperiled Promise: The State of History in the National Park Service*. The report challenged the National Park Service to pursue loftier goals than simple self-preservation through "instill[ing] ownership in the NPS mission." The OAH urged parks to "embrace possibilities for larger societal change" in their interpretive work. Parks, in their vision, should be places of engaging with fellow citizens to understand the many different viewpoints inherent in American society today. "The power of civic engagement," the authors urged, "is that it provides a means for engaging the dynamic and contested worlds beyond park boundaries. Indeed, the most exciting possibilities for civic transformation emerge at points where staffers and visitors encounter difference—from their own worlds, their own times, their own experiences."[1]

"By identifying injustices and exploring solutions," the authors urged, "cultural institutions can fulfill what one historian [Roehampton University's John Tosh] calls 'the principle function of historical debate,' namely, 'to keep open an awareness of alternatives.'" By engaging visitors in broad-ranging dialogue, the OAH believed that the National Park Service could help build critical civic skills: "the ability to uncover and surface assumptions, to suspend judgement, to experience equality among participants, to listen attentively, to practice empathy, to embrace multiple perspectives, and to use the knowledge of past conflicts to inform these processes."[2]

Assessing the efficacy of interpretive programming in the field, Dr. Marc J. Stern (Virginia Tech) and Dr. Robert Powell (Clemson University) came to a similar conclusion: to remain relevant, the core National Park Service communication styles must change. Of the over 370 interpretive programs audited, 73 were at Civil War associated sites—about 20 percent of the total sample data. Stern and Powell measured programming using a key metric for success, akin to the one advocated for by the OAH: visitors were explicitly asked how likely an interpretive experience was to change their behavior.[3]

The study categorized interpreter communication styles into three categories—friend, authority figure, and walking encyclopedia—and assessed the effectiveness of each. They found that of all the modes of communication Park Service interpreters utilized, the "walking encyclopedia" identity type, which focuses "on conveying a large volume of facts," was least likely to inspire behavior change in visitors. But, in spite of its ineffectiveness at accomplishing twenty-first-century interpretive goals, National Park Service interpretation skews strongly to this mode of communication. Stern and Powell found that 75 percent of all National Park Service programming exhibited the "walking encyclopedia" identity as their primary mode of delivery. National Park Service programming used the least effective tool the most often.[4]

As the National Park Service was beginning to confront its outdated and ineffective communication style, it was forming a deeper partnership with the International Coalition of Sites of Conscience. Formed in 1999 by Ruth Abrams, director of the Lower East Side Tenement Museum in New York City, the coalition initially included three National Park Service sites. Their goal was simple and revolutionary: they set out to make museum spaces sites of healing. "We hold in common the belief," the group's founding document declares, "that it is the obligation of historic sites to assist the public in drawing connections between history interpreted at our sites and the contemporary implications." Cultural institutions should make "promoting humanitarian and democratic values . . . a primary function."[5]

Partnering with the coalition in 2012, the Interpretive Development Program, Washington's interpretive training arm, offered classes and resources to help stimulate deep and meaningful dialogue on modern social issues in historic landscapes. "The coalition intends," *National Parks* magazine explained in 2000, "to explore complex historical issues, including sexism, racism, totalitarianism, immigration, genocide, and poverty." Though it took them a decade to realize it, the National Park Service and its Civil War sites matched that description of modern echoes within the past almost perfectly. For Ruth Abrams, and increasingly for the National Park Service, the aim of shifting interpretation to a discussion about modern issues was an obvious strategy to help audiences find meaning and relevance. "What we are simply trying to do is to use history to think about the present."[6]

The final key to a shift in communication style was the realization by the broader National Park Service community that the Civil War's sesquicentennial celebration came at the same moment as the semicentennial of the American civil rights movement. This was not immediately clear in 2009, as then–National Capital Regional (NCR) Director Peggy O'Dell led a team to define a vision for the commemoration. The initial vision was for the Park Service to serve as a purveyor of facts and figures. It intended for rangers and staff to primarily "serve as a respected, reliable source of diverse perspectives on the war and its lasting effects." The efforts to move to a social understanding of Civil War landscapes, although grossly needed, was still almost wholly focused in retrofitting a social past into the story of the military past, instead of looking to help visitors confront the stormy present.[7]

This vision shifted radically in the summer of 2011, even after the commemoration had begun. In a draft of a new service-wide interpretive plan, pushing National Parks Service sites and units to integrate the Civil War and the civil rights struggles into one larger, more meaningful narrative, the goal began to take shape with distinct clarity. The purpose of the combined commemoration should not simply be education and transfer of factual information from the ranger to the audience. Instead, parks had the distinct responsibility to help visitors "commemorate America's greatest historic events beginning with the Civil War," not as events isolated in time, but "as a point of departure for an examination and exploration of the on-going quest for legal and social equality for all Americans, the still-vigorous debate over the appropriate reach of the federal government, and the never ending effort to reconcile differing cultural values held under a single national flag." The commemoration should be just as much about the present, the National Park Service's national and regional leadership was beginning to realize, as it was about the past.[8]

The Power of Intentionally Changing the Narrative: Vicksburg and Gettysburg

The National Park Service's commemoration of the Civil War sesquicentennial was an uneven affair. It was typified by triumphs and missteps, glimmers of a relevant future for interpretation, and missed opportunities to ask powerful questions about today's society. No two sets of commemorative events seem to capture that divide better than those mounted by Vicksburg and Gettysburg National Military Parks.

Cathy Beeler served as the first National Coordinator for the Civil War sesquicentennial, organizing events on behalf of the Director's Office in Washington, DC, Beeler helped propel forward Signature Events, which were the backbone, national-caliber. She helped provide funding to parks looking to innovate and create meaningful experiences.[9]

Beeler's position helping each park plan their event was not without missteps. Michael Madell, the superintendent at Vicksburg, was one of those who pushed back on Beeler. He did not want to waste money on a ceremony, which no one would remember moments after it ended. Madell admitted that the racial and cultural divide in Vicksburg, where Medgar Evers had crusaded for civil rights just five decades before, was a great chasm. "Because of where we are," he told Beeler, "there are very few people in this community who have probably ever been in this park. They don't care that we're a National Park. A lot of people don't come here."[10]

Beeler saw the opportunity; she challenged Vicksburg to do something that would matter. When Madell raised the objection that it would cost hundreds of thousands of dollars, Beeler waived the objection aside. She eventually secured more than $400,000 from the Washington office's budget and in matching funds of $400,000 to make Madell's dream of becoming relevant to his community possible.[11]

At other times, Beeler ran into institutional resistance. At a planning meeting for the Gettysburg Signature Event, the committee tried to decide on who the park and partners should court as a keynote speaker. "They were initially looking at celebrities," Beeler recalled. She piped up with her suggestion: Oprah Winfrey. "You could just see jaws drop at that point."[12]

Someone around the table broke the silence. "Well you'd have every black housewife around show up for that," they intoned, "but I don't know how many Civil War buffs would show up." That, of course, was Beeler's point. Inviting someone like Oprah Winfrey would open up that Civil War landscape to an entirely new audience in a visionary way. The traditional Civil War audience was guaranteed to attend an event as central to the war's memory as Gettysburg. But the call fell on deaf ears. "The body language at that point," Beeler recalled, "you could see arms crossed, people leaned back in their chairs." The message was abundantly clear to the national coordinator: "that was the last planning meeting I was invited to for a while."[13]

After the opening ceremonies, where keynote speaker Doris Kearns Goodwin made a valiant if somewhat hamfisted attempt to link the battle in 1863 with the evaporation of voting rights in 2013 and the modern civil rights struggle for LGBTQ rights (and was panned by conservative critics for doing so), a caller contacted C-SPAN from Santa Ana, California. "As I was watching the program with interest and the camera was going around the audience, I didn't see any African American people there," the caller, Rachel, commented. "Wasn't the Civil War fought for their freedom? . . . Why didn't we see any or why didn't I see any?"[14]

Historian and Gettysburg College professor Peter Carmichael was quick to answer the query. "Just imagine, you're an African American person who comes to Gettysburg and what was one of the songs played this evening?" he asked, answering with the pained, "Dixie." The

Figure 6.1. An African American visitor wearing a Declaration of Independence shirt and waving a "Let Freedom Ring" flag at the Angle at Gettysburg as Confederate reenactors and visitors "retreat" across the field of Pickett's Charge at the 150th anniversary. Photo by author

event and the town were still not welcoming in new audiences by changing expectations and offering vibrant, different programming. The framework for the commemoration, with keynote historians and exclusively white dignitaries giving speeches, was not enough of a shift in tone. "For many people who come to the town of Gettysburg, who see [on the shops on Steinwehr Avenue] Confederate flags," the professor sharply criticized, "that immediately sends a message to them: I'm not welcome here, this is not my history." No amount of keynote speeches could fix that sense of open hostility.[15]

Gettysburg's mirror twin in Vicksburg, on the other hand, eschewed one grand celebration. They took their signature event money and spread it across a few events in April and May of 2013. The Vicksburg Heritage Fair took Civil War history off of the battlefield and into the local community, with a keen eye toward engaging diverse communities by making sure their faces were represented by reenactors and their stories were part of the narrative. By the end of the month, the park had hosted three open-air concerts aimed at broadening appeal to audiences, many African American, who may have never set foot on the battlefield. "They involved the community and the community loved it," Cathy Beeler remembered, "they had local choirs that they brought in. They brought in an African-American choir." The Jackson Mass Community Choir, along with members of the MADDRAMA theatre troupe from Jackson State University (Vicksburg's nearby HBCU), sang gospel ballads and patriotic songs and performed a dramatic retelling of the story of Vicksburg's citizens during the siege.[16]

"That place was packed," Beeler recalled. "There were people standing and clapping their hands and singing on a battlefield." Superintendent Maddell turned to Beeler, both of them crying at the sight, and said, "If you would have told me that we could have brought this part of our community into the park and have them singing and clapping their hands on this ground, I never would have believed it. This was worth it."[17]

Shuffling the Cards and Stories to Be Inclusive: Trading Card Program

The shift in mission for the commemoration had an immediate impact. At the beginning of the inaugural celebration, in the spring of 2011, the Northeast Region and National Capital Region partnered to launch a series of Civil War trading cards aimed at engaging youth audiences and helping entice them to become stewards of the parks. These trading cards, featuring a blue-and-gray background and green text, were not unlike the interpretive materials, which might have been handed out in the parks for decades. Twenty-three parks drafted text and submitted photos for a total of 189 cards.[18]

"The Battle of Antietam, fought on September 17, 1862, was the bloodiest single day battle in American history with over 23,000 soldiers killed, wounded, or missing," the text of a typical card read "This battle and its aftermath had a profound impact on those who fought here, the people of Sharpsburg, and the course of American history." The card does not even attempt to probe the why or how of the impacts the battle might have had on American history. Of the nine cards initially created by Antietam National Battlefield, only one mentioned emancipation (almost randomly fronted by a November 1863 photograph of Abraham Lincoln) and one focused on the citizens of Sharpsburg.

Similarly, the three cards created by Civil War Defense of Washington failed to mention the civilian population at all. Absent were the thousands of escaped slaves seeking refuge behind the fortress circle. They instead focused on military movement and nothing else. On Ford's Theatre National Historic Site's cards, Lincoln's role in shifting the focus of the war toward emancipation and black citizenship, a role that ultimately got him killed by white supremacist John Wilkes Booth, is not mentioned at all. "He was the first president to put his picture on a campaign button," Lincoln's card tells visitors, "the only president to hold a patent, and the only president to have stood on a battlefield during ongoing battle."

The following year the program changed greatly as it went national—guided by the shift in ethic toward diverse stories. "By the end of the commemoration," the Park Service reported at the end of the commemoration, "over 90 parks provided more than 600 different cards with unique and diverse stories about the historic and ongoing struggle for freedom and equality for all Americans." The second run of cards, and the parks that participated, was far different than the first.

At Shiloh National Military Park, the cards showed how a Civil War landscape could deftly walk the line, incorporating the traditional and the radical in equal measure. Alongside cards dedicated to Confederate general Albert Sidney Johnston and Union general Ulysses S. Grant, the park also included Andrew Jackson, an African American laborer wounded at Shiloh and who later was a member of the 55th Massachusetts Infantry. Stones River National Battlefield skillfully integrated the military history of the war within its larger context. One card featured a formerly enslaved local man, William Holland, who became a sergeant in the US Colored Troops. Holland eventually became a local landowner who, the park aptly and poignantly described, had moved "from property to property owner." Even the cards confronting traditional military history themes were peppered with diverse meanings. The card on Fortress Rosecrans was not simply a dry recitation of the fort's dimensions. Instead, it drove deeper: "For the people of Murfreesboro, Fortress Rosecrans loomed as a grim reminder that the Union Army controlled their town."

The expansion of the cards to embrace the new theme of Civil War to civil rights also brought new parks and stories into the narrative. Jean Lafitte National Historical Park distributed cards with the gravestone of Sergeant Walker Cole, a soldier in the United States Colored Troops, which discussed the one hundred black veterans of the Civil War buried in the Chalmette National Cemetery. They also distributed cards with a photo of young black girls escorted to and from school by US Marshals, highlighting how the struggle of the Civil War was an "ongoing struggle for equality" and how four six-year-olds desegregated New Orleans' public schools in 1960.

The National Park Service drew an important lesson from the initial failure to encompass diverse stories and its eventual success. "The CW2CR Trading Card Program was immensely popular," the NPS concluded in their after-action report. "However, in the process of researching and articulating its many stories, the agency became more keenly aware of its own unconscious bias." The National Park Service was still fighting the penchant, both in its staff and its organizational culture, to ignore large swaths of the American experience. The

Civil War to civil rights transition, however, "created a heightened awareness of this issue," and a much-needed sense of urgency among leadership.[19]

Open to Seeing Your Own Stumbling: Selma to Montgomery NHT

In March of 2015, as Civil War sites were planning their programming for the end of the sesquicentennial, Selma to Montgomery National Historic Trail in Alabama was preparing for its fiftieth anniversary celebration. Park staff embraced the words shared by Representative John Lewis and President Barack Obama at the commemoration of Bloody Sunday at the Edmund Pettus Bridge. According to Lewis: "We come to Selma to be renewed. We come to be inspired. We come to be reminded that we must do the work that justice and equality calls us to do."[20]

President Obama was likewise looking for renewal, to be a witness to a moment of change. "There are places and moments in America where this nation's destiny has been decided," he told the crowd as he stood facing the NPS's new Selma Interpretive Center. "We know the march is not yet over. We know the race is not yet won. We know that reaching that blessed destination where we are judged, all of us, by the content of our character requires admitting as much, facing up to the truth."[21]

Selma to Montgomery NHT's Superintendent Sandy Taylor and Chief of Interpretation Tim Sinclair crafted a different sort of commemoration than those which had preceded it in the Civil War to Civil Rights commemorative calendar. Instead of a speakers' colloquium or a "typical" roster of ranger programs at historic sites, the site organized a massive "Walking Classroom," focused on dialogue and discussion of civil rights in a current context. The event was opened to college students and adult activists from across the United States; over two hundred participants ended up re-creating the fifty-four-mile march from Selma to Montgomery over the course of five days from March 20 to 25. The reenactment was not aimed at historical authenticity. Participants wore modern hiking shoes and carried signs proclaiming their desire for equal rights for LGBTQ citizens or immigrants. Park rangers led discussions along the march with participants, connecting the social activism of the 1960s back to the legacy of slavery in the 1860s and forward to modern struggles for civil rights today.

The event was transformative for both the marchers and the National Park Service. It typified exactly what the revolution in interpretation fomenting for two decades had been striving toward. The march, one participant remembered, "was one of the most powerful experiences of my life. . . . From the very first step, it was clear that we were walking on holy ground." The reverence was undergirded, however, with a large dose of modern relevance. "Tim [Sinclair] and the other rangers made sure we understood the history, respected the sacrifices of the first foot soldiers and martyrs, and challenged us to make the connections between the past and the present." She repeated the mantra that became the rallying cry of the whole group: "What's your Selma?"[22]

The event's turning point came on March 24th. The previous day, the National Park Service arranged for more porta-johns to follow the marchers—a simple logistical choice with resonant effect. When the bathrooms were delivered, Park Service staff casually announced

Figure 6.2. Participants walked, hobbled, and rolled the fifty-four miles from Selma to Montgomery carrying flags and signs in this effective five-day combination of reenactment, living history, and protest event commemorating the voting rights movement's climactic moment. Photo by author

that some were for men and some were for women. Ivy Hill, one of the marchers, posted to a marcher-organized Facebook page that night that they "need[ed] to tell y'all about why I was disheartened this afternoon when there was an announcement about the restrooms being gendered." For Ivy, who identifies as genderqueer, even going to a bathroom can create a moment of stress. "One of the difficult things I have to face on a daily basis as a gender nonconforming person," they wrote that night, "is gendered restrooms. I'm regularly told I'm in the wrong bathroom regardless of which bathroom I use." Hill knew what they were asking was big, but also crucial. "I get that these conversations can be really hard," they wrote that night after the march, but the fact was that they "have to have them almost daily. . . . And when we avoid those conversations we are contributing to the erasure of trans* identities."[23]

Hill was not just noting the damage caused by the moment, but demanding accountability. "I have an ask for you," Hill told their fellow marchers. "If there is not an announcement about gender neutral restrooms made in the morning please make it a point to talk to your rangers about why gender neutral restrooms are important. It sure would mean a whole lot to me to know that y'all have my back too." The community poured out their commitment to hold the National Park Service staff to task if nothing was done. Sylvia Strobel expressed thanks to Hill, noting she too was growing thanks to the experience. "Some of us are still in the learning process," she encouraged Hill. "Have patience with us. You are loved."[24]

The ultimatum was not necessary in the slightest. The National Park Service staff understood the heavy reality of the fact that, in an event commemorating a fight for equality, they had easily and thoughtlessly perpetuated systemic inequality. The staff used that as a moment of personal and agency growth. The next morning, Tim Sinclair stood in front of the assembled group and addressed the issue. Rachel Faber Machacha remembered as Sinclair "modeled authenticity and vulnerability in so many ways, all while being extremely professional in carrying off a huge undertaking." He announced that the restrooms would be gender-neutral from that moment on.[25]

But he did more than fix the problem. He apologized on behalf of himself, the staff, and the National Park Service for stepping on someone else's Selma. Sinclair's "brand of respectful, big-hearted, resourceful professionalism," Machacha noted, "should be replicated everywhere." More than a year and a half later, Ivy Gibson-Hill, now married to their partner who marched from Selma to Montgomery along their side for the right to love whoever they wanted, remembered that the "NPS was amazing. A shining example of what growth should look like."[26]

From Tokenism to True Partnership: A Radical Departure at Appomattox

As the Civil War to Civil Rights commemoration evolved and shifted, it became clear that to remain relevant the National Park Service needed to move away from token gestures and toward true integration, appreciation, and willingness to adapt and change in response to diverse stories. This can be seen in two commemorative moments in Virginia, which bookended the celebration.

At the opening of the Civil War sesquicentennial, the sweltering battlefield at Manassas played host to Virginia's first signature event. The temperatures climbed into the triple digits as National Park Service Director Jon Jarvis, Virginia Governor Robert McDonnell, and a variety of other dignitaries gathered on the rostrum behind the park's visitor center. Before the speeches, the crowd was led in the Pledge of Allegiance. William Howell, chair of the Virginia Sesquicentennial of the American Civil War Commission, introduced the speakers who would lead the audience: "Please remain standing for the Pledge of Allegiance to the flag, which will be led by Colonel Richard Robinson and descendants of James Robinson, who in 1861 owned much of this land."[27]

The gesture was massive, but went completely unnoted. James Robinson was a free African American man who owned land and a home near the crest of the hill where General Thomas J. Jackson stood like a stonewall and the Confederacy won its first crashing victory. His wife was enslaved. His children were enslaved. Two of his sons, James and Alfred, had been sold into the Deep South and the New Orleans hellish slave market. Alfred returned finally in 1888; James was never heard from again. The audience never heard any of these details, none of these resonances. When the Robinson family was brought to the microphone to lead the audience in a full-throated celebration of their citizenship, the audience was never confronted with the fact that James Robinson himself was not accorded the rights of a citizen as the battle raged on his farm. The gesture was entirely token.[28]

At the end of the entire Civil War to Civil Rights commemoration, the events at Appomattox Court House National Historical Park were a marked departure from the tokenism of the Manassas commemoration. At the commemoration of the surrender of Robert E. Lee's army in 1865, the causes, context, and consequences of war were on clear and full display, impossible for any visitor to miss. Amid the typical centennial-style events of salutes and reenactments of the surrender, the park mounted a unique event.

Arising from a partnership with the Carver-Price Legacy Museum, a local African American historical society that focuses on the history of segregated education in Appomattox, the event sought to link the end of the war with the beginning of a much larger struggle. "The two groups got along so well," the *Lynchburg News and Advance* reported shortly after the event, "they decided to keep meeting and develop a program focusing on slavery as part of the sesquicentennial commemoration." The story of one woman, Hannah Reynolds, caught the entire group's imagination.[29]

Hannah Reynolds was the only known civilian casualty of the battles around Appomattox Court House just before the surrender of Lee to Grant. Reynolds, along with 4,600 other men, women, and children in Appomattox County, began the day enslaved but ended it free thanks to the stroke of the pen in Wilmer McClean's parlor and a salute between two generals. "This program," the park told its guests, "invites us to think about emancipation as one of the significant outcomes of the war. Unlike the theoretical ideas that inspired the Emancipation Proclamation, Lee's surrender led to Emancipation Realized." The park made the event the pivot point of their commemoration, seizing upon and subverting one of the potent memes of Civil War commemoration in the early twenty-first century: luminaries. A meme within Civil War commemorations, candles in paper bags have often been used to help highlight the toll of war. Antietam places luminaries on their battlefield in December, a drive-through Christmas light-show illustrating every soldier killed, wounded, or missing in the battle. Gettysburg and Fredericksburg likewise adorn the graves of the dead in their cemeteries with these votives at commemorative events.[30]

But Appomattox's subversion of the symbol was almost a complete 180-degree switch from their use in other Civil War sites. The candles were no longer for soldiers, but for citizens. They were no longer markers of sorrow, but ones of promise. Lining the main thoroughfare through the historic landscape, the park lit "4,600 luminaries representing each emancipated person in Appomattox County as a result of the surrender."[31]

Down the road between the candles, the park and the local African American community conjured a potent image: a funeral for Hannah Reynolds. Reenactors eulogized the slave-turned-citizen. The Reverend Al Jones III, a member of the local schoolboard, portrayed Flemming Johnson, an African American pastor from 1865. "When I think about Hannah, I think about her going to heaven through Africa and it makes me want to sing," he said in character to the gathered audience of over a thousand visitors. The funeral featured the Footsteps to Freedom Mass Choir and a smaller choir from the Diamond Hill Baptist Church in Lynchburg. They sang gospel hymns. They prayed over Hannah's "body." The living historians conjured their own scene, researched and orchestrated largely with their own effort, of suffering and hope in April of 1865. The crowd was invited to "join the procession in song, and help us light 4,600 luminaries!"[32]

Timothy Corbett, who helped organize the event, said it changed him. "I like the feeling of living this experience," he told the Lynchburg newspaper. "Now, when I come to this park, it means more to me. Otherwise, it wasn't that significant to me as an African American." And Park Ranger Ernie Price, who helped orchestrate the National Park Service's events, admitted as much to the audience. "Even after 125 years, we still weren't ready to embrace the legacy of emancipation," he told the crowd, highlighting that emancipation was small acts, like funerals and the ongoing struggle for civil rights in America. "Slavery's end," he told the crowd, "was not just the work of a president, a battle, a surrender, or even a war." It took a true partnership, not one specially created to mount an event, but an honest, open, and equal friendship between two groups, to create the successful inversion of the norm that ended the Civil War commemoration at Appomattox.[33]

Finding Sudden Relevance: Charleston, 2015

On the evening of June 17th, 2015, after the parades and celebrations of the Civil War 150th were largely over, a young man stepped into a church in Charleston, South Carolina. Just a few years before, cannonfire and grand Confederate balls had underlined how America wanted to remember the Civil War and its legacy. Now Dylann Roof, a twenty-one-year-old white supremacist, violently submitted his own voice to the narrative. He entered the Emanuel African Methodist Episcopal Church and gunned down in cold blood nine praying victims. And suddenly, America was confronted with the question that most had failed to ask for the past half-decade: what does the Civil War mean to America today?

Pictures of Roof carrying Confederate flags and drawing white-nationalist slogans appeared across the Internet. One of the places he chose to visit in the months leading up to the horrendous murders was Sullivan's Island, where the National Park Service preserves Fort Moultrie, a bastion connected to the beginning of the Civil War in 1861 and where, the service estimates, 40 percent of the slaves brought to North America first set foot on the continent. To a large extent, Roof was a Park Service visitor: looking for meaning in a landscape. He sketched "14-88," a neo-Nazi slogan, onto the sand at the beach and had his photograph taken in front of the marker commemorating the importation of human chattel.[34]

The gravity of the moment took time to settle on the National Park Service. But the damage done in the prayer meeting in Charleston hit hard. One employee at Fort Sumter National Monument realized that, had she chosen to go to the prayer meeting at her home church that night, she might have been killed as well. Another man of color realized he was working at Fort Moultrie the day that Roof visited and worried what the next hateful visitor might do to him. Still more employees were friends with State Senator Clementa C. Pinckney and others who had been murdered while they prayed. It took a groundswell from African American employees in the Charleston area and beyond advocating for their neighbors' well being to finally get action. It was a short but pointed struggle to convince the upper tiers of the National Park Service why someone outside of Charleston, someone outside that park or that region of the Park Service, should care about the issues at hand. Ranger and community partnership specialist Michael Allen, who worked closely with the murdered Pinckney in a bid to diversify Park Service stories and sites in Charleston, helped elevate the voices of park staff to the national leadership in Washington.[35]

And, after intense prodding, the Agency finally acted. In a memorandum to his employees after the shooting, National Park Service Director Jon Jarvis looked to the potential of parks as a solution to the pain caused in Charleston and around the country. "As we have seen with other recent tragedies, national parks can be places of healing and reconciliation for communities torn apart by violence."[36]

Jarvis was harkening to the local Park Service responses to protesting and civil unrest in the St. Louis, Missouri, area after the killing of Michael Brown in the suburb of Ferguson. "NPS staff at the arch in St. Louis quickly realized that people would need a safe place to express their feelings," a later NPS report explained. "They immediately issued a permit for people to demonstrate peacefully in front of the Old Courthouse, where *Dred Scott v. Sanford* was heard in 1857, and where people have gathered throughout history to advocate for change." But the park employees also stepped into other roles beyond safe space, literally becoming safe teachers. With schools closed because of protesting in the streets around St. Louis, "rangers helped teach at informal 'Peace Schools' at libraries and other locations to help students learn more about the history of racism and how it relates to today." By stepping into the moment of healing, the rangers found themselves in a new persistent role as community organizers, healers, and stewards, continuing "to work with the schools and the police force toward better communication and understanding."[37]

As he helped his employees face the new challenge at Charleston, Director Jarvis called not for just individual action but a concerted effort. "Many of our NPS sites and programs are dedicated to telling the stories of our on-going struggle for freedom and equality," he admitted, highlighting just how central the modern act was to the historical themes the National Parks steward. "I want to recognize this role that we play to help our nation heal," the director wrote. An understanding of parks as sites of healing in the present moment and overcoming the misdeeds of both the present and the past was beginning to take root at all levels of the service. "This is an essential part of our responsibility to the special places in our care," the director continued, "and to the civic process that makes this nation great."[38]

The Social Purposes of Civil War Sites

If the goal of interpretation is to impel visitors to think anew and act anew, the best tools an interpreter has to provoke such a shift are being woefully underutilized. The visitors' voices themselves, joining the discussion of what the past means in their daily lives, might be the crucial piece now missing in the relevance of Civil War landscapes. During the National Park Service's interpretive offerings for the Civil War sesquicentennial, the events and programs that saw the greatest success integrated diverse voices. Some unearthed them from the past and highlighted them in meaningful ways, like the second phase of the Trading Card program to decent success. Some created programming by National Park Service staff *about* diverse groups. But the greatest success came from the moments of true partnership and collaborative construction, with more success flowing from a greater ability for parks to relinquish control of their spaces to the visitors themselves.

Having parks as sites of social conscience and civic engagement is not necessarily new, but extremely necessary in a fractured world. A rote recitation of history might be a noble pursuit. An explication of even the motivations of the men on the field might be worthwhile. But in an ever-diversifying nation with easier access to fonts of information and primary sources, those functions will necessarily become increasingly irrelevant. Parks can, however, step into a broader societal role: that of civic uplift. Indeed, why waste tax dollars on an institution like the National Park Service if it does not, in some real, concrete way, act as a force to make our broader society a better place? From the Constitution's preamble on, the US government's stated goal and purpose has always been the forging of a healthier, more just and free society.

All of this points to the need for a new, continual reconciliation. It demands an ongoing process of probing the national wounds we've left festering and doing the hard, continual work of binding and rebinding them. These sites do not simply need to remain places of rote knowledge transfer, but can become places where we listen to our fellow citizens' grievances and resolve to do better next time. Just as the Common Core educational revolution refocused the goal of education on a student's capacity for critical thinking and analysis, this shift in interpretation refocuses its goals on building civic capacity and an active engagement with democracy.

History is only meaningless chronicle without the actions it inspires us to perform in the present. Learning facts is not enough. These landscapes demand more of us. The men killed in fratricidal combat, the women enslaved and raped, the children chewed by dogs and blown apart by bombs demand that we set out to build civic capacity and empathetic citizens. Provoking citizens to meaningful action in the present is the true potential of America's historic hallowed ground.

Notes

1. Anne Mitchell Whisnant et al., *Imperiled Promise : The State of History in the National Park Service* (Bloomington, IN: Organization of American Historians, 2011), 114–17.
2. Anne Mitchell Whisnant et al., *Imperiled Promise : The State of History in the National Park Service* (Bloomington, IN: Organization of American Historians, 2011), 114–17.
3. Marc J. Stern, Robert Powell et al., "Identifying Best Practices for Live Interpretive Programs in the United States National Park Service," (2012) [accessible at https://goo.gl/0iUJ72], 3–4, 25.
4. Marc J. Stern, Robert Powell et al., "Identifying Best Practices for Live Interpretive Programs in the United States National Park Service," (2012) [accessible at https://goo.gl/0iUJ72], 15–16, 29, 32.
5. William A. Updike, "Museum Coalition to Promote Democracy," *National Parks* Vol. 74, No. 7-8 (July/August 2000), 18–19.
6. William A. Updike, "Museum Coalition to Promote Democracy," *National Parks* Vol. 74, No. 7-8 (July/August 2000), 18–19.
7. National Park Service, "Appendix B: CW150 Vision Statement and Goals," *Civil War to Civil Rights Commemoration Summary Report* (2016), 93.
8. "Draft Service-Wide Interpretive Plan Commemoration and Celebration of the American Experience in Pursuit of Freedom," 15 August 2011.
9. Cathy Beeler, interview with the author, 12 October 2016.
10. Cathy Beeler, interview with the author, 12 October 2016; Appendix to CW2CR Report.
11. Cathy Beeler, interview with the author, 12 October 2016; Appendix to CW2CR Report.
12. Cathy Beeler, interview with the author, 12 October 2016.
13. Cathy Beeler, interview with the author, 12 October 2016.
14. "Open Phones with Peter Carmichael," C-Span, 30 June 2013 [available at: https://www.c-span.org/video/?313031-15/open-phones-peter-carmichael&start=803].
15. "Open Phones with Peter Carmichael," C-Span, 30 June 2013 [available at: https://www.c-span.org/video/?313031-15/open-phones-peter-carmichael&start=803].
16. Rick Martin, "Press Release: Memorial Day Weekend Concert," 17 May 2013 [available at: https://www.nps.gov/vick/learn/news/memorial-day-concerts-2013.htm]; Cathy Beeler, interview with the author, 12 October 2016.
17. Cathy Beeler, interview with the author, 12 October 2016.
18. The NPS Civil War Trading Cards have been aggregated in a Flickr account at flickr.com/photos/tradingcardsnpsyahoocom. Although these cards all use the second layout scheme, the text for the original run of Northeast Region and National Capital Region cards is largely intact from their initial print run.
19. National Park Service, *Civil War to Civil Rights Commemoration Summary Report* (2016), 87.
20. John Lewis, "Introducition of the President," 7 March 2015 [http://www.cnn.com/TRANSCRIPTS/1503/07/cnr.06.html].
21. Barack Obama, "Remarks by the President at the 50th Anniversary of the Selma to Montgomery Marches," 7 March 2015 [https://www.whitehouse.gov/the-press-office/2015/03/07/remarks-president-50th-anniversary-selma-montgomery-marches].
22. Patricia Templeton as quoted in National Park Service, *Civil War to Civil Rights Commemoration Summary Report* (2016), 5.

23. Ivy Hill, post in "50th Anniversary Selma to Montgomery Walking Class Events" Facebook Group, 23 March 2015.

24. Ivy Hill, post in "50th Anniversary Selma to Montgomery Walking Class Events" Facebook Group, 23 March 2015.

25. Rachel Faber Machacha, "Be Swift, My Soul, To Answer Him! Be Jubilant, My Feet!," *Ain't gonna let nobody turn me around* (blog), 26 March 2015, https://rachelfabermachacha.word press.com/2015/03/26/be-swift-my-soul-to-answer-him-be-jubilant-my-feet/.

26. Rachel Faber Machacha, "Be Swift, My Soul, To Answer Him! Be Jubilant, My Feet!," *Ain't gonna let nobody turn me around* (blog), 26 March 2015, https://rachelfabermachacha.word press.com/2015/03/26/be-swift-my-soul-to-answer-him-be-jubilant-my-feet/; Ivy Gibson-Hill, interview with the author.

27. "Battle of Bull Run 150th Anniversary Commemorative Ceremony," C-Span, 21 July 2011 [available at: https://www.c-span.org/video/?46812-1/battle-bull-run-150th-anniversary -commemorative-ceremony&start=223].

28. Manassas National Battlefield Park, "Resource #1: Biography of James Robinson," *War for Freedom: African American Experiences in the Era of the Civil War* [https://www.nps.gov/mana/learn/education/upload/Res1_JamesRobinsonBio.pdf].

29. Katrina Koerting, "Hundreds gather in Appomattox for living history event addressing scars of slavery," *The News and Advance* (Lynchburg, VA), 12 April 2015.

30. National Park Service, *Civil War to Civil Rights Commemoration Summary Report* (2016), 104.

31. National Park Service, *Civil War to Civil Rights Commemoration Summary Report* (2016), 104.

32. Katrina Koerting, "Hundreds gather in Appomattox for living history event addressing scars of slavery," *The News and Advance* (Lynchburg, VA), 12 April 2015.

33. Katrina Koerting, "Hundreds gather in Appomattox for living history event addressing scars of slavery," *The News and Advance* (Lynchburg, VA), 12 April 2015.

34. Justin Miller, "Dylann Roof Visited Slave Plantations, Confederate Landmarks," *The Daily Beast*, 20 June 2015, [http://www.thedailybeast.com/articles/2015/06/20/dylann-roof-visited -slave-plantations-confederate-landmarks-before-massacre.html].

35. Keena Graham, interview with author, 22 November 2016; Paul Bowers, "A Park Service expert weighs in on the Confederate flag," Charleston City Paper (Charleston, SC) [http://www.charlestoncitypaper.com/charleston/a-park-service-expert-weighs-in-on-the-confederate -flag/Content?oid=5268513].

36. Jonathan Jarvis to All NPS Employees (internal memorandum), 19 June 2015.

37. National Park Service, *Civil War to Civil Rights Commemoration Summary Report* (2016), 80.

38. Jonathan Jarvis to All NPS Employees (internal memorandum), 19 June 2015.

CHAPTER 7

Commemoration, Conflict, and Constraints

The Saga of the Confederate Flag at the South Carolina State House

W. Eric Emerson

FOR NEARLY EIGHTY YEARS major commemorations of the Civil War served as a catalyst for decisions regarding the display of the Confederate battle flag on South Carolina State House grounds.[1] In 1938 a first-term state legislator introduced a House resolution to drape a Confederate flag behind the Speaker's desk. The resolution, which passed with little notice or fanfare, coincided with the seventy-fifth anniversary of the Civil War and introduced a Confederate flag as an official symbol of the state for the first time in the twentieth century.[2] Over twenty years later, another legislator successfully petitioned to fly a Confederate battle flag over the State House to mark the Civil War centennial.[3] The flag's final removal from the State House grounds in 2015 would coincide with the closing of the Civil War sesquicentennial, although a greater catalyst was the racially motivated murder of nine church parishioners in Charleston.[4] The Confederate flag's presence at the State House drew little attention for decades; by the end of its time there it had become the source of widespread national debate.

The still unresolved saga of South Carolina's public display of Confederate flags can provide historical organizations with a number of lessons. It demonstrates the powerful role that commemoration can play in the public use of contested historic symbols. It also provides insight regarding how conflicts over highly politicized objects or symbols can force historical organizations into a form of paralysis, which makes them bystanders or witnesses until asked to contribute. Ideally historical organizations educate the public, inform conversations regarding controversial objects, and navigate the more rancorous aspects of debate. Fears of decreased funding or support, however, can negate those capabilities. At a time when increasing contention and a lack of civility characterize most debates, those historical organizations that are able must be true to the collective mission, drawing upon knowledge of the past to offer perspective and depth to these discussions, while still maintaining professional objectivity.

An Ascendant Banner

The saga of the Confederate flag at the South Carolina State House began on March 2, 1938, when Representative John D. Long (1901–1967) introduced House Resolution 1954, which resolved that the Clerk of the House secure a US flag, a South Carolina flag, and "a Battle flag of the Southern Confederacy" to drape behind the Speaker's desk.[5] Long's efforts to display the Confederate flag coincided with the peak of the Civil War's seventy-fifth anniversary and an intensified public interest in the war following publication of Margaret Mitchell's *Gone with the Wind* (1936) and Douglas Southall Freeman's four-volume *Robert E. Lee: A Biography* (1934–1938).[6] Long's gesture also preceded a series of commemorative events in Columbia including a joint annual meeting of the United Confederate Veterans (UCV) and Sons of Confederate Veterans (SCV) and the dedication of the General Robert E. Lee memorial tree and the General Robert E. Lee highway marker at the State House on August 30, 1938.[7] Long's resolution also followed heated debate in Congress regarding an Anti-Lynching Bill advocated by President Franklin D. Roosevelt.[8]

Eighteen years later Long was elected to the South Carolina Senate, and on April 10, 1956, he introduced Resolution S. 749, which was to "provide for the draping of the Battle Flag of the Southern Confederacy in the Chamber of the Senate of the State of South Carolina." Unlike his House resolution eighteen years earlier, Long's Senate resolution drew upon language found on later Confederate monuments. It stated that "the Battle Flag of the Southern Confederacy inspires our dedication to the resurrection of truth with glorious and eternal vindication." Resolution S. 749, like the 1938 House resolution, was adopted by the members of the Senate "on immediate consideration."[9]

Long's newest resolution to display the Confederate flag coincided with planning for the war's centennial. On September 7, 1957, President Dwight D. Eisenhower signed legislation creating the Civil War Centennial Commission (CWCC). Two years later Long joined the national advisory council for the CWCC and served on that body until 1964.[10]

Long's second resolution also followed a period of intense opposition in the General Assembly to the Supreme Court's *Brown v. Board of Education* ruling, which struck down school segregation. Long, a vocal opponent of federal interference in the states' business, made a number of speeches to that effect prior to offering his resolution to display the Confederate flag.[11]

By the beginning of the Civil War centennial, South Carolina had another leading advocate for the Confederate flag's display. John Amasa May (1908–1976), a native of Graniteville and resident of Aiken, had served several terms in the House by the beginning of the Civil War centennial. Whereas Long embraced the Confederate flag for both commemorative and political reasons, May was an avid Civil War buff and an active member of the Sons of Confederate Veterans. Referred to as "Mr. Confederate," May had a passion for all things Confederate including uniforms, which he wore in the House. When South Carolina created the South Carolina Confederate War Centennial Commission (SCCWCC), May was chosen as its leader. Long would later serve as a member.[12]

Although similar, May and Long had very divergent opinions regarding the centennial. May believed that it could unite the nation at a time of growing disunity, while Long viewed the centennial as yet another opportunity for the South to be vilified. Long predicted that northerners and the federal government would use the commemoration to "damn our good name forever beyond repair."[13] In contrast May and the members of the SCCWCC hoped events in Charleston surrounding the one-hundredth anniversary of the firing on Fort Sumter would launch a successful national centennial commemoration.

Civil rights issues ultimately derailed May's plans. Racial segregation prevented African American members of the New Jersey and Missouri commemorative delegations from lodging with whites at the Francis Marion Hotel in Charleston. After rancorous debate between state delegations, the SCCWCC, and the CWCC, President John F. Kennedy made available accommodations at the Charleston Naval Station. Kennedy's action resulted in two sets of commemorative events: one attended largely by the southern delegations in Charleston, and one mostly attended by the northern delegations at the Charleston Naval Station. Newspapers referred to the confrontation as "the second battle of Fort Sumter."[14]

Influenced by the growing controversy in Charleston, May refocused his attention on Columbia and requested that a Confederate flag be flown over the State House in observance of centennial activities being held in Charleston. There was little opposition to the banner's placement. Daniel Hollis, the last surviving member of the SCCWCC, later commented, "I was against the flag going up . . . but I kept quiet and went along. I didn't want to get into it with the UDC [United Daughters of the Confederacy] girls." By Tuesday, April 11, 1961, a Confederate flag was flying from a flagpole on the State House roof.[15] The display was intended to be temporary and to coincide with the one-hundredth anniversary of the firing on Fort Sumter, but May took steps to ensure that a flag would be placed there for a much longer period.

On February 14, 1962, May and Representative F. Julian LeMond of Charleston introduced Concurrent Resolution H. 2261 "requesting the Director of the Division of Sinking Funds and Property to have the Confederate Flag flown on the flagpole on top of the State House." The resolution passed the House and went to the Senate, where it was referred to the Senate Judiciary Committee. One month and one day later, Senate Judiciary reported favorably on H. 2261 and returned it to the House with concurrence on March 20, 1962. On March 28, 1962, a local newspaper published a picture entitled "Three Flags Flying," which showed the Confederate Battle Flag flying beneath the US and South Carolina flags on the State House dome. The resolution did not specify a time limit for flying the flag.[16]

Figure 7.1. The South Carolina Legislative Manual for 1963 showing the Confederate flag flying from the State House dome at the height of the Civil War centennial. South Carolina General Assembly, House of Representatives, Office of the Clerk, Legislative Manuals, 1963, S165091. South Carolina Department of Archives and History, Columbia, South Carolina.

The conclusion of the Civil War centennial marked the end of the first phase of South Carolina's flag saga. Long, who introduced the Confederate flag into the House and Senate chambers, died two years later in 1967.[17] May, who worked to increase the banner's visibility outside the State House, died in 1976 in Aiken.[18] His, and the centennial commission's most controversial, legacy, however, remained visible for decades. Of the Confederate flag flying from the State House dome, SCCWCC member Hollis would later comment, "It just stayed up. . . . Nobody raised a question."[19] Over the next four decades, more than a few questions would be raised.

Flag of Contention

By the end of the Civil War centennial in 1965, federal legislation, including the Voting Rights Act (1965), was facilitating the gradual re-entry of African Americans into the political process in South Carolina. Between 1902 and 1969 no African Americans held state office. In 1969 two African Americans were elected as judges. In 1970 James L. Felder, I. S. Leevy Johnson, and Herbert U. Fielding were elected to the South Carolina House of Representatives, and in 1983 the Reverend I. DeQuincey Newman became the first African American in the 20th century to be elected to the State Senate.[20]

The election of African Americans brought a new and very different voice and perspective to the display of the Confederate flag. The first small stirrings of outside opposition to the flag occurred in the late 1960s, and in July 1972 the YMCA, NAACP, and other organizations called for the flag's removal from the State House.[21] Over the next several years the chorus of opposition grew. In February 1980, the House killed two bills aimed at removing the Confederate flag from the State House.[22] In 1987 the Southeast Region of the NAACP passed a resolution calling for the removal of the Confederate flag from the State House domes in South Carolina and Alabama and the removal of the Confederate flag from the Georgia and Mississippi state flags.[23] In 1993 the mayors of Columbia and Charleston called for the flag's removal and a number of State House bills were filed dealing with the issue.[24] South Carolina Attorney General T. Travis Medlock issued an opinion concluding that "there currently exists no binding legal authority to fly the Confederate flag on the State House dome" and stating that the State House Committee had the authority to remove the flag and should do so. His successor, Republican Charlie Condon, came out against Medlock's decision in 1994 and promised to take measures to see the flag re-raised on the State House if it was removed.[25]

The most important product resulting from the 1994 debate was a compromise deal crafted by the Senate and entitled the Heritage Act of 1994. Senators Glenn McConnell, John Courson, and Verne Smith (all SCV members) met with African American senators including Kay Patterson, Robert Ford, Maggie Glover, and Darrell Jackson and with Representative Joe Brown, head of the Legislative African American Caucus. Together they crafted a plan that would remove the Confederate flag from the State House dome, place a square Confederate battle flag at the Confederate Soldiers Monument in front of the State House, and place a Confederate First National Flag at the UDC Monument. The act also called for language in the legislative record explaining reasons for the flag's display and legal protection of Confederate monuments throughout the state. The legislative session ended, however, without the plan's adoption.[26]

The summer of 1996 saw a turn in the flag saga. Governor David Beasley signed a bill authorizing the erection of an African American Monument on State House grounds, making it the first of its kind in any of the fifty states. Beasley also had a change of heart regarding the Confederate flag. Previously he claimed that the flag "represents a heritage to celebrate—not racism." Following the burning of a number of African American churches throughout the South, Beasley announced that the flag should be removed and the Heritage Act of 1994 adopted, which came as a great surprise to both politicians and citizens.[27] Beasley later commented that he believed the flag issue would lead to his defeat in the following election, and he was correct. In 1998 James H. "Jim" Hodges, the House minority leader, bested Beasley in the gubernatorial election, which marked the first time in twelve years that a Democrat had been elected governor.[28]

Though Hodges owed his victory largely to African American voters, he made a pledge to Confederate heritage groups that he would take no action regarding the flag. The NAACP, however, had other ideas. In July 1999 it called for an economic boycott of South Carolina that was scheduled to begin on January 1, 2000, but which was in effect by October 1999.[29] The economic impact on the state was marginal, but the public relations impact was great. Media attention focused even more closely on South Carolina as Hodges, who attempted to remain neutral regarding the flag, began meeting with legislators. In December 1999, 51 of the 67 surviving members of the 1962 legislature that had voted to raise the flag advocated for its removal, and they were joined by former governors. In response 6,000 flag supporters marched to the State House in January and displayed the largest Confederate flag in the world as part of a rally labeled "Heritage Celebration 2000." Anti-flag forces countered by launching a protest march called "King Day at the Dome," which occurred on the Reverend Martin Luther King Jr.'s birthday and attracted more than 40,000 attendees.[30]

In his State of the State Address, Governor Hodges called for the flag's removal. He offered a plan that adopted many of the provisions of the Heritage Act of 1994 in addition to recognizing the birthday of Dr. Martin Luther King Jr. and Confederate Memorial Day as state holidays.[31] Legislators failed to offer legislation in support of Hodge's plan, but a large group of the state's historians joined business leaders, the NAACP, and various political groups who called for the flag's removal. In early April Charleston Mayor Joe Riley led a group of over 2,000 marchers from that city to Columbia in a call to remove the flag. Dubbed "Get in Step," the march was joined by Governor Hodges when it arrived in Columbia.[32]

After years of debate, protests, and legislative maneuvering, the General Assembly finally made the decision to deal with the flag in a manner that they hoped would resolve the issue forever. The Senate crafted the Heritage Act of 2000, which would remove the Confederate flag from the State House dome and the House and Senate chambers and would place a square Army of Northern Virginia Confederate battle flag on a flag pole at the Confederate Soldiers Monument. The bill also recognized Dr. Martin Luther King Jr.'s birthday and Confederate Memorial Day as state holidays and prevented the removal, disturbance, or alteration of any monuments or memorials erected on the state's public property. Governor

Hodges signed the Heritage Act and many South Carolinians breathed a sigh of relief and on July 1, 2000, two Citadel cadets, one African American and one white, removed the flag from the State House dome. Confederate flags also were removed from the House and the Senate.[33] A square Confederate battle flag was raised from a thirty-foot flagpole behind the Confederate Soldiers Monument. Thousands of pro- and anti-flag demonstrators gathered to witness the event and hurl insults at each other.[34] Both sides in the flag debate were left feeling that they had been wronged terribly. Little would change for the next ten years, but the Civil War sesquicentennial and tragic events would bring the flag back into the public consciousness.

Murder and Reckoning

Dylann Roof thrust the controversy about the battle flag back into the public spotlight following the murder of nine members of a Bible study at the Emmanuel African Methodist Episcopal Church in Charleston on June 17, 2015.[35] As South Carolina mourned the victims, attention quickly focused once again on the Confederate flag flying at the State House. The day after the murders, Governor Nikki Haley ordered the state's flags to fly at half staff. Observers quickly pointed out that the Confederate flag at the Confederate Soldiers Monument was not at half staff. The reason why was obvious for anyone who looked closely at the banner. To prevent the flag's removal by protestors, the flag pole was not equipped with a pulley system. Instead it was secured by two clips that prevented it from flying at half staff. The flag could only be removed from the pole, an act that would require approval by two-thirds of the General Assembly as outlined in the Heritage Act of 2000.[36]

On June 20 President Barack Obama and national Republican notables including former governors Mitt Romney and Jeb Bush and senator Ted Cruz called for the flag's removal. On June 22 Governor Nikki Haley, flanked by a number of notable South Carolina politicians of both parties including US Republican senators Lindsey Graham and Tim Scott, and numerous former governors including David Beasley and Jim Hodges, called for the state legislature to remove the flag.[37]

On July 6 the South Carolina Senate took up debate to remove the Confederate flag from the Confederate Soldiers Monument. After considerable discussion, the bill passed by a vote of 37–3. Political observers were not surprised by the one-sided vote. The most prominent victim of the shooting was Senator Pinckney. He had shared a desk with Senator Vincent Sheheen, a two-time Democratic nominee for governor, who had advocated for the flag's removal during his most recent gubernatorial campaign. Sheheen therefore sponsored the bill to remove the flag.[38] The Senate had lost one of their own to the actions of a deranged racist, and it was undoubtedly in their minds that Pinckney had been a vocal opponent of the flag flying on State House grounds. The Senate therefore voted overwhelmingly to honor the memory of their friend.

The House debate on the Senate's bill began on July 8 and lasted nearly thirteen hours. The debate became increasingly acrimonious as the night progressed. As in 2000, pro-flag legislators offered a large number of amendments to the bill with the hope that they could return it to the Senate for more debate. As early morning approached, one representative declared that she was an ancestor of Jefferson Davis (an assertion later brought into question by genealogists). She made an impassioned plea for the flag's removal and tearfully declared that not removing the banner would be "adding insult to injury" to the widow and children of Senator Pinckney. Finally, at 1:00 AM on July 9, the House voted 94 to 20 to pass S. 897. Governor Haley signed the legislation at 4:00 PM the same day and provided for the legal removal of the last Confederate flag on State House grounds.[39]

On July 10, 2015, hundreds of spectators gathered at the Confederate Soldiers Monument. Some carried Confederate flags, but the majority had gathered to celebrate the flag's removal. At 10:00 AM, a detachment of uniformed officers from the South Carolina Highway Patrol marched to the flag pole and lowered the banner as many in the crowd cheered and sang. The lowered banner was folded with military precision and handed to Department of Public Safety Director Leroy Smith, one of two African American cabinet members. Smith then handed the banner to Allen Roberson, director of the Confederate Relic Room and Military Museum. It remains there to this day.[40]

Debate regarding the appropriate display of the last flag continues. On June 29, after the murders but before the flag was removed, the Confederate Relic Room issued a fiscal impact estimate of $1,020,000 for housing and displaying the flag.[41] Afterwards the House drafted legislation directing the Relic Room to "establish and maintain an appropriate, permanent, and public display honoring South Carolina soldiers killed during the Civil War to include the South Carolina Infantry Battle Flag of the Confederate States of America." The legislation also tasked the Relic Room's director with projecting costs associated with the display and reporting them to the House Ways and Means Committee by January 1, 2016.

On December 22, 2015, the SC Confederate Relic Room delivered a feasibility study to the Senate Finance Committee and the House Ways and Means Committee developed jointly by the director, architects, and a design firm. It called for expanding the museum and opening a new, second-floor exhibit gallery to display the last Confederate flag to fly on State House grounds in a memorial setting that commemorates South Carolina soldiers who died in the Civil War. The overall cost was $3,627,250 with $550,000 for the soldier memorial and flag exhibit. It would include a glass case containing the flag flanked by three eight-foot tall panels comprised of tiny LED screens. These would display the scrolling names of the 22,000 South Carolinians killed in the war, digitized photos from the museum's collection, videos, and other items. The plan also called for additional annual operating funds for the Relic Room totaling $234,172.[42]

The release of this estimate generated significant debate in the media and the public. Before substantive legislative debate could take place regarding the proposals, the House Ways and Means Committee suggested a proviso to study moving the Relic Room from Columbia to Charleston. The plan was intended to increase the institution's visibility and attendance, but it met with opposition from Charlestonians. The Senate agreed with the proviso, but Governor Haley vetoed the proposal as duplicative of a Facilities Management Study (2013) of all state properties. Today, the last Confederate flag to fly on State House grounds remains stored in the vaults of the Relic Room. There are no plans to display it in the near future.

Commemoration as Catalyst and Constraint

National commemorations of the Civil War have played a notable role in the ongoing saga concerning the display of the Confederate flag on public property in South Carolina. Of the six incidents involving movement of the Confederate flag around the State House, five took place immediately prior to, during, or immediately following a major commemoration of the Civil War. The only incident that does not fit this pattern, the removal of the flag from the State House dome to the Confederate Soldier's Monument in 2000, occurred after the airing of Ken Burn's award-winning documentary *The Civil War*, which sparked a period of widespread public interest in the war.[43]

Commemorative periods provide an excellent opportunity to teach and learn about the past, but they also serve as a vehicle for people to remember events through a particular lens. Education, family lore and legend, as well as racial and personal perspective can shape how an individual or group views key historical events. For white and native-born members of the General Assembly from 1938 to 1962, who voted to introduce the Confederate flag to the State House and moved it to more prominent positions there, the flag's presence reinforced a familiar narrative of the war that they learned both in school and through family lore.[44] It also served as a symbol of pride and resistance against forces that sought to change South Carolina.

Conversely, the 150th commemoration preceding the flag's removal from State House grounds emphasized slavery, emancipation, gender, and the war on the home front. These perspectives challenged Lost Cause interpretations and provided a very different view of the war and its outcomes. Therefore the story of the Confederate flag at the South Carolina State House is a tale of two different views of the past and how societal changes affected the public display of this particular symbol.

Commemorations not only remind people of the past, they also provide a vehicle for nostalgia and the veneration of events, symbols, and persons. Such was the case with the 75th, 100th, and early days of the 150th anniversaries of the Civil War, when Confederate heritage organizations played a significant role. In 1938 Long wished to see the Confederate flag displayed in the House chambers for a variety of reasons, but his resolution coincided with the peak of the last major Civil War commemoration in which surviving veterans actually participated. It also was a precursor to the national meeting of Confederate heritage organizations in Columbia and Confederate monument dedications on State House grounds. Similarly May's efforts to raise the banner above the State House in 1961 and 1962 undoubtedly were a by-product of his position as Chair of the SCCWCC and his membership in the SCV. Nearly fifty years later South Carolina Confederate heritage organizations sponsored a Secession Ball in Charleston on December 20, 2010, to "celebrate" Secession, which sparked widespread media attention, demonstrations, and protests. The flag's final removal from the Confederate Soldiers Monument in 2015 can be attributed partially to the weakened state of the same organizations, which were unable to offer any significant resistance through the General Assembly.

Although actions regarding the Confederate flag's introduction on State House grounds coincided with commemorative periods, they also coincided with a period of racial segregation and voter suppression that was not challenged until the mid-twentieth century. As federal opposition to South Carolina's racial policies mounted, the Confederate flag moved to progressively more prominent positions in and on the State House dome.

The political nature of the Confederate flag debate significantly influenced how commemorative and cultural organizations dealt with the subject. In 2008 the General Assembly created the South Carolina Civil War Sesquicentennial Advisory Board (SCCWSAB) to lead the state's 150th commemoration. It was comprised of political appointees, representatives of public and private cultural institutions and agencies, employees of the National Park Service, and members of Confederate heritage organizations. Its diverse membership sought harmony during meetings and avoided discussion of the Confederate flag to maintain unity. This self-censorship extended beyond the SCCWSAB. In statewide public meetings regarding how the war should be commemorated, few participants addressed the banner at the State House.[45]

Throughout the debate regarding the public display of the Confederate flag at the State House, flag opponents argued that it belonged in a museum, and each of the Confederate flags removed from State House property was transferred to state-funded museums. In 2000 the flag removed from the State House dome and the two flags displayed in the legislative chambers were transferred to the South Carolina State Museum, the state's largest museum. The Heritage Act of 2000 dictated that the flags be "permanently displayed in a suitable location in the State Museum." The museum was free to determine the nature and location of the display.

The State Museum's curatorial staff members advocated for a Confederate flag display that would interpret the banners in the wider context of the Civil War and public remembrance. The politically charged nature of the flags and financial concerns resulted in a modest exhibit with minimal interpretation on the museum's fourth floor. There the three flags were displayed together with captions and a single interpretive panel. The exhibit has not changed since its unveiling.[46]

When the Confederate flag was removed from the Confederate Soldiers Monument in 2015, it was transferred to a different state-funded museum. Established by the UDC in 1896, the Confederate Relic Room and Military Museum is the state's third oldest museum and is located in the same building as the State Museum. Legislation removing the flag from the Confederate Soldiers Monument also called for the flag's "appropriate display." Legislators conveyed their expectations for the display to the Relic Room's director, and plans for the banner were a by-product of those conversations. In those plans the last Confederate flag to fly on State House grounds would be the focal point of a display, which would serve as a memorial to the more than 22,000 South Carolina Civil War soldiers who died in the war.[47]

The last Confederate flag to fly at the State House is quite different from other items in the Relic Room's collections. It is a printed nylon banner manufactured in the United States, with a retail value of less than $52 at the time that it was purchased by the General Services Division.[48] In contrast the Relic Room houses and displays Confederate flags that were carried in battle. These banners are displayed and interpreted as art in a minimalistic style, and each banner's history and significance is made available to researchers upon request.[49]

The eventual fate of the last Confederate flag to fly at the State House rests with the General Assembly, which must determine an appropriate amount to spend on its display.

The General Assembly controls funding for all state agencies and commissions and has always determined the location of Confederate flags on state-owned property. Acknowledging this reality, state-funded cultural organizations have attempted to limit their comments regarding the flag or its history. The Civil War sesquicentennial followed the Great Recession, which resulted in devastating budget cuts for many state agencies. Faced with the threat of further reduced funding and mission effectiveness, South Carolina organizations were loath to risk engagement in politically charged issues.[50]

During the 2015 flag debate, "it belongs in a museum" was a common refrain used by many who wished to remove the flag from the public sphere.[51] As public historians we can view this statement in one of two ways. We can regard it as an acknowledgment by stakeholders that only historical institutions are equipped to curate and interpret controversial objects. We also can interpret "it belongs in a museum" as a throwaway phrase that does little to answer the most challenging questions facing our institutions: how will the contested object be interpreted, and how will it be funded? With the Confederate flag in South Carolina, the answers to both of those questions are politically charged.

Regardless of how we interpret "it belongs in a museum," our profession compels us to display, contextualize, and interpret artifacts of the contested past in an informative and objective manner. By doing so we confirm the public's confidence in our unique capabilities and educate people about historical events or periods that represent the widest breadth of the human experience, not just the joyous or triumphant.

With our calling before us, it is incumbent upon willing organizations to serve as leaders when the public is searching for answers regarding the contested past. Such leadership necessitates a proactive and bold assertion of our profession's unique ability to provide the public with a framework for understanding contested objects and to properly contextualize them in the form of wayside markers, digital exhibits, or more traditional museum displays.

The proliferation of social media has accelerated this process. The public can quickly focus on a historical topic, and public history organizations must be nimble and capable of adapting to and influencing opinion at critical moments. They also must be able to develop compelling plans for interpretation, which they can rapidly and enthusiastically offer to stakeholders. Failure to act decisively will result in our organizations either being overlooked or forced to cope with outcomes that run counter to our missions. The Confederate flag saga in South Carolina illustrates this last point.

Because of the extended, decades-long conflict over the public display of the Confederate flag in South Carolina, few state organizations, other than the Confederate Relic Room, will wish to interpret the Confederate flag and its greater significance in the near future. The Relic Room houses one of the largest collections of Confederate flags in the world and has over a century of experience collecting, preserving, and exhibiting banners. It has at its disposal the last artifacts of the flag saga in South Carolina, including the last Confederate flag to be removed from the State House grounds in 2015, and three other flags removed from the State House in 2000 that are housed in the same building.

It also has other advantages. As the General Assembly's chosen repository for the last banner, the Relic Room could launch an exhibit regarding the long and contested history of the Confederate flag and do so with far less negative attention than any other state institution. Heritage organizations and pro-flag citizens, who already support the Relic Room, would welcome an exhibition that focuses on the flag. The greatest challenge for the Relic Room would be to attract visitors who oppose the flag and what they believe it represents. The name of the museum alone is enough to deter some visitors, who otherwise could benefit from viewing a comprehensive exhibition regarding the history of the Confederate flag on State House grounds.

The only way to overcome this reticence would be to diligently ensure that the exhibit tells as much of the story as possible. It should begin with the banner's wartime origins, briefly explaining the reasons for the war (as outlined in South Carolina's Declaration of Immediate Causes) and then explain the practical need for flags to identify troops, in this case Confederate, in battle. The exhibit would need to explain the furling of Confederate banners at the war's conclusion and the finality denoted by that act. It would then need to address the Confederate battle flag's use by the Ku Klux Klan as an act of terror during and after Reconstruction. An exhibit should discuss the repatriation of Confederate and Union flags as an act of healing between the North and South in subsequent years. It also would need to outline the flag's history as both a commemorative symbol and as a symbol of opposition to civil rights during the mid twentieth century, and its place as a cultural symbol of the New South. In each panel or display it would be paramount to juxtapose the uses of the banner with the impact on those whom it was intended to intimidate, challenge, or affect. In essence the exhibit would provide a comprehensive history of the flag.

An exhibit also should trace the history of anti-flag efforts, highlighting the efforts of legislators and citizens who worked to have it removed from the public sphere. Since many people on both sides of the issue survive, such an exhibit would benefit from the recorded voices or transcriptions of interviews with those who actively worked for the flag's continued presence or removal from State House grounds. Because the 2015 murder of parishioners at Emanuel AME Church led to the flag's removal from the Confederate Soldiers Monument, the exhibit would need to address that tragic event and its impact on the flag debate. The logical ending to an exhibit would be an interactive display that would record visitors' opinions about the flag, either through written messages or through brief, recorded or filmed comments. This exhibition should be thorough, balanced, and ultimately lead to a greater understanding of this historic symbol, which continues to resonate in the present and will continue do so in the future. Though daunting, such an exhibit is already being contemplated among historical administrators in South Carolina.[52]

The time for such a display, however, is not now. Only two years have elapsed since the removal of the last Confederate flag from State House grounds, and we cannot yet evaluate the importance of the flag saga to South Carolina history. Was it merely a sideshow or distraction as the state wrestled with larger issues, or was it the milestone event declared in the media? History is like fine wine; we can only appreciate its complexities through the passage of time. More time must elapse before we can provide a reasonably accurate assessment of the saga's significance to South Carolina's past and future.

In the interim, however, we must look to those topics that provide insight regarding the origins of popular veneration for the Confederate flag. Today organizations from around the state and nation are looking at the Reconstruction period to provide some of the answers. In addition the American Association for State and Local History is leading a movement to reconsider all Confederate monuments and place names in a campaign that aims in part to remove from the historic landscape objects and words deemed by some to be offensive.[53] Although it would be easy to argue that such actions are antithetical to historic preservation, this focus is not surprising. Public historical institutions are working diligently to assert relevance in a twenty-first-century digital world dominated by STEM initiatives.[54] Having witnessed the public uproar regarding the Confederate flag debate during the summer of 2015, it makes sense that historical organizations would wish to assume the mantle of leadership in a similar movement to remove Confederate monuments.

Ultimately though, such endeavors are being led by historical organizations that do not risk significant reductions in funding or reprisals for their efforts. The flag saga in South Carolina has demonstrated that state-funded cultural organizations are in no position to lead on most highly-politicized issues. They will, however, be forced to play a significant role in any efforts to alter the historic landscape by removing Confederate monuments. Many state archives and historic preservation offices are legislatively mandated to protect the historic landscape, and they undoubtedly will undertake that responsibility even if it leads to direct conflict with other public history organizations. During these interesting times, we may be on the verge of a "civil war" of sorts within our own field. We can be assured, however, that it will be far more "civil" than the war that continues to capture the public imagination and drive our collective passions over 150 years later.

Notes

1. For a history of the Confederate flag in South Carolina through 2000, see K. Michael Prince, *Rally 'Round the Flag, Boys!* (Columbia: University of South Carolina Press, 2004).
2. *Journal of the House of Representatives of the Second Session of the 82nd General Assembly of the State of South Carolina Being the Regular Session Beginning Tuesday, January 11, 1938*, vol. 1 (March 2, 1938), 784.
3. *Journal of the House of Representatives of the Second Session of the 94th General Assembly of the State of South Carolina Being the Regular Session Beginning Tuesday, January 9, 1962* (March 20, 1962), 458, 962.
4. "Confederate Flag Comes Down on South Carolina's State House Grounds," *Washington Post*, July 10, 2015.
5. *Journal of the House*, March 2, 1938, 784.
6. Robert J. Cook, *Troubled Commemoration: The American Civil War Centennial, 1961–65* (Baton Rouge: Louisiana State University Press, 2007), 17.
7. Dennis E. Todd, *Sons of Confederate Veterans in South Carolina, 1894–2000* (Columbia: South Carolina Division Sons of Confederate Veterans, 2001), 39.
8. Prince, *Rally 'Round the Flag*, 28–29.
9. *Journal of the Senate of the Second Session of the 91st General Assembly of the State of South Carolina Being the Regular Session Beginning Tuesday, January 10, 1956* (April 10, 1956), 1184–85.
10. Cook, *Troubled Commemoration*, 18–30; Prince, *Rally 'Round the Flag*, 37; Bailey, Morgan, and Taylors, eds., *Biographical Directory of the Senate*, 950.
11. Cook, *Troubled Commemoration*, 77–78.
12. Prince, *Rally 'Round the Flag*, 36–37; Todd, *Sons of Confederate Veterans*, 48.

13. *Address by the Honorable John D. Long on the South Carolina Secession Ordinance Delivered before the Senate of the Ninety-Third General Assembly of the State of South Carolina*, May 27, 1960.

14. Prince, *Rally 'Round the Flag*, 39–44; Cook, *Troubled Commemoration*, 88–119.

15. *The State* (Columbia), April 12, 1861; Brett Bursey, "The Day the Flag Went Up," http://scpronet.com/point/9909/p04.html, accessed January 25, 2017, 3.

16. *Journal of the House*, March 20, 1962, 962; *The Columbia Record*, March 28, 1962.

17. *The State* (Columbia), May 20, 1967.

18. Todd, *Sons of Confederate Veterans*, 20.

19. *Ibid.*

20. Walter Edgar, *South Carolina: A History* (Columbia: University of South Carolina Press, 1998), 541, 562.

21. *The State* (Columbia), July 30, 1972.

22. *Journal of the House of Representatives of the Second Session of the 103rd General Assembly of the State of South Carolina*, vol. 1 (January 16, 1980), 280–86.

23. Prince, *Rally 'Round the Flag*, 138–39.

24. *Ibid.*, 141–42.

25. *The State* (Columbia), October 19, 1993; *Ibid.*, 144.

26. *The State* (Columbia), May 28, 1994; Prince, *Rally 'Round the Flag*, 162–63.

27. Prince, *Rally 'Round the Flag*, 180–83.

28. "South Carolina and the Confederate Flag-An Online Discussion with Former Governor David Beasley" (February 14, 2000), accessed January 25, 2017, http://www.washingtonpost.com/wp-srv/liveonline/00/politics/beasley0214.htm; *Ibid.*, 198.

29. *The State* (Columbia), October 17, 1999.

30. Prince, *Rally 'Round the Flag*, 205–206, 212–13; *Greenville News*, December 8, 1999; *The State* (Columbia), January 9, 2000; *The State* (Columbia), January 17, 2000.

31. *The State* (Columbia), February 13, 2000.

32. *Ibid.*, April 2–8, 2000.

33. *The State* (Columbia), May 23, 2000.

34. *Ibid.*, July 2, 2000.

35. *Post and Courier* (Charleston), June 17, 18, and 19, 2015.

36. *Washington Post*, June 19, 2015; *New York Times*, June 19, 2015.

37. *The State* (Columbia), June 22-24, 2015.

38. *The State* (Columbia), July 6, 2015.

39. *The State* (Columbia), July 9, 2015; *Post and Courier* (Charleston), July 14, 2015; Brooks D. Simpson, "A Descendent of Jefferson Davis? A Question for Jenny Anderson Horne," *Crossroads*, accessed January 25, 2017, http://crossroads.wordpress.com.

40. *The State* (Columbia), July 10, 2015.

41. Interview with Allen Roberson, Director, Confederate Relic Room, January 25, 2017.

42. *Ibid.*

43. Chris Mackowski, "The Ken Burns Effect," *Emerging Civil War*, September 11, 2015, accessed January 31, 2015, https://emergingcivilwar.com/2015/09/11/the-ken-burns-effect/.

44. Due to the efforts of Mary Simms Oliphant, South Carolina children used William Gilmore Simms's *History of South Carolina* (1840, 1842, and 1860) as their textbook for much of the twentieth century. Simms Initiative, accessed January 25, 2017, http://simms.library.sc.edu/view_item.php?item=121755.

45. W. Eric Emerson, "Report on the Activities of the South Carolina Civil War Sesquicentennial Advisory Board (In keeping with provisions of SC Code 60-11-150 through 60-11-180)," December 31, 2016, S108214, Reference Files of the Civil War Sesquicentennial Advisory Board, South Carolina Department of Archives and History.

46. Interview with Fritz Hamer, Curator of History and Archives, South Carolina Confederate Relic Room, January 25, 2017.

47. Interview with Allen Roberson, Director, Confederate Relic Room, January 25, 2017.

48. Interview with Rachel Cockrell, Registrar, South Carolina Confederate Relic Room, January 5, 2017.

49. Interview with Allen Roberson, Director, Confederate Relic Room, January 25, 2017.

50. *Ibid.*

51. "White House Says Obama Believes Confederate Flag Belongs in a Museum," *Reuters*, June 19, 2015; "Confederate Flags Belong in Museums: Our View," USA Today, accessed January 25, 2017, http://www.usatoday.com/story/opinion/2015/06/23/south-carolina-haley-confederate-flag-shooting-editorials-debates/29166303/.

52. Interview with Allen Roberson, Director, Confederate Relic Room, January 25, 2017.

53. "Reconsideration of Memorials and Monuments," *History News: The Magazine of the American Association for State and Local History*, Autumn 2016.

54. *History Relevance Campaign*, accessed January 25, 2017, https://www.historyrelevance.com/.

CHAPTER 8

Getting to the Heart

The Intersections of Confederate Iconography, Race Relations, and Public History in America

Dina Bailey and Nicole Moore

FOCUSING ON THE INTERSECTIONS of Confederate iconography, race relations, and public history in the United States is essential in current discussions surrounding Confederate flags, memorials and monuments. Without acknowledging the strong tie between the legacies of race and the Confederacy, arguments will never be resolved. And, as stewards of the past, we must step back and consider our own motivations and what roles we have played and can play in community reconciliation. This chapter will set the groundwork for looking past the immediate arguments in order to work toward long-term solutions for our communities. There is a lasting impact that can be won through greater awareness, authentic dialogue, and a commitment to change.

Stewards of the Past

History organizations are the stewards of the past, both history *and* memory, and provide connections between the past and the present. This is one of our most important roles as history organizations and one of the seven core values of history. The History Relevance

Campaign affirms, "By bringing history into discussions about contemporary issues, we can better understand the origins of and multiple perspectives on the challenges facing our communities and nation."[1] Just as it is important to provide historical contexts as part of current interpretations of the past, it is equally important to acknowledge the contemporary influences that we (as human beings) consciously and subconsciously tie to our historical interpretations. Perhaps the first step is to recognize that there is no true objectivity in regards to discussions about history.

Intellectually, that makes sense. Emotionally, this can be a difficult pill to swallow. The Civil War, and what has been entwined with it before and after, is probably still the most hotly contested event in American history. It is not only the event that is contested, but the memories and emotional baggage that continue to pull at our heartstrings generations later. As history organizations internally debate whether or not to step into the political fray of Confederate iconography, we must grapple with a spectrum of potential actions and reactions. In this chapter, we will use "Confederate iconography" in the broadest possible terms to mean anything that symbolizes connections to Confederate history (including memorials, monuments, flags, etc.). What role should history organizations play in discussions of what to do? Is it even the place of history organizations to play a role at all? Should we provide a platform for free speech? Should we provide a safe haven for genuine dialogue? Should we be activists, advocates, or silent observers? And, whatever actions we do or do not take, how will that impact our staff, our volunteers, and our communities? The questions may seem infinite. As a field made up of passionate individuals, with a clear responsibility to the past, present, and future, we stand at a crossroads. It is an intersection at which we have stood time and again; hopefully, this time, we have the courage to face the emotionality tied to the intersections of Confederate iconography, race relations, and public history.

While our current intersection has similarities to those of the past, there are several differences. Perhaps the most noticeable difference is the existence of Black Lives Matter, a national activist movement that has proven to be a sustained force of influence. Black Lives Matter was created in 2013 following George Zimmerman's acquittal for the shooting death of Trayvon Martin. Since then, those tied with the movement (either officially or unofficially) have been visible, both physically and digitally, during a number of tense racial events throughout the United States. Responses from this segment of the black community have become swifter and louder in the past decade. That said, Black Lives Matter has also been criticized. Some are critical of the movement's tactics, others question the movement's lack of focus on intra-racial violence, and the phrase "All Lives Matter" has sprung up in response to the Black Lives Matter movement causing yet another divide.

Within our present context, there is no prescriptive answer to how to move forward or which direction our field will take at this intersection. With that said, we have the opportunity to stand strong together and loudly proclaim our belief that relevant history is *inclusive* history and that supporting the increase of empathy in our communities can only make the world a better place. This cannot be done if we, as individuals, are not willing to look deeper into what we've generally accepted as the standard interpretation of historical events. It cannot be done if we refuse to look into our personal motivations, biases, and truths. And, it cannot be done if we refuse to take personal and professional risks in our current social and political climates. While not the only subject we could use for these personal and professional analyses, an examination of the intersections of Confederate iconography, race relations, and public history offers us an opportunity to reflect on the profound impact that historical interpretation has on us as individuals and as professionals.

Standing at the Intersection

For those willing to step into this potential quagmire and for those who have already taken the step, let us begin with a seemingly simple question: How did we come to be at this particular crossroads? This won't be a chapter where we focus on the history of Confederate iconography or race relations in the United States. It won't be about the generally accepted "facts" that make up American history or the motivations of those who created the memorials that have become contentious today. Instead, let us quickly agree to the basic understanding that there is a fragmentary nature to the past. As history professionals, we put together the pieces of the puzzle as best we can while ultimately realizing that we will never have the full puzzle and that the pieces we do have are colored by a number of things, such as the context of the times, the collected pieces of the puzzle (archival documents, artifacts, oral histories, etc.), and the personal motivations and biases of those who participated in and/or researched the past. We should also agree that the past is complicated and that human beings have a tendency to distill these complications into a more basic and palatable understanding. And, finally, let's accept that human beings are emotional; no matter how much we try to allow our intellect to lead, we feel hurt, anger, embarrassment, shame, pride, and a host of other emotions tied to our individual pasts as well as the pasts of our communities, regions, and other demographic affiliations. Woven into all of this is the instinct for some to rush toward confrontation and for others to step away from it.

With those basic premises, it really shouldn't be a surprise that we continue to stand at the point where the past and present collide, where we decide again and again how we will react to the subjectivity of the past. But, of course, here we stand surprised by the reactions of colleagues, neighbors, and fellow citizens when contemporary events conspire to force these uncomfortable discussions. While an empirical study hasn't been completed, discussions across various public history associations support the premise that many of those affiliated with history are keeping silent, perhaps fearing that any statement will alienate someone within their constituency; yet, silence ends up reverberating just as loudly through the spectrum of a community's stakeholders. Many history professionals want to narrow Confederate iconography to a discussion of artifacts and interpretive labels, to whether the artifact should remain on display or not and what the sign should or should not say. It's a comfortable space for us; we believe that we have the experience and expertise to shine in this role. And, we *want* to shine. There are also institutional restraints partially determined by the possibility of alienating donors or even potential donors. Others want to broaden the focus of the discussion to a reflection of the specific time period in which the artifacts came to be. If we do this, we begin to allow for a critique of the people who surrounded the artifacts. But, with this, we continue to firmly concentrate on the past without acknowledging the shade that is provided by years of connected legacies and our own messy human emotions. On the other end of the spectrum, a good number of individuals and institutions are ready to act in a way that makes a strong contemporary statement, agreeing with William Faulkner, who declared that "the past is never dead. It's not even past."[2] This contingent would also probably agree with Pierce Brown, who additionally connected justice to the past when he wrote that "justice isn't about fixing the past; it's about fixing the future. We're not fighting for the dead. We're fighting for the living. And, for those who aren't born yet."[3]

So, the next logical questions (after how we got here) delve into why we are fighting and for what we are fighting. Don't accept the simplest, most comfortable answers to those questions. We are fighting for our identities and we are fighting because who we are determines where we stand in connection to others (no matter the context). In the context of race relations in the United States, the fight has had victories and losses for both sides over hundreds of years. Even in that statement, we must revise our thinking to allow for more complexity. The reality is that there have never only been two sides. Race in America has always been about shades of grey and the privileges and restrictions that come with those ever-mutating shades. The continued fight has, sometimes literally, been about survival. Can we blame anyone for a desire to maintain his or her sense of self? To naturally want to keep whatever they perceive as the status quo or to rise above their perceived current status? Encouraging mindful empathy begins with releasing blame and guilt.

Now, that gets into an uncomfortable space for a significant number of history professionals. Many of us cringe to even think about touching the emotional triggers that therapists, social workers, and activists connect to on a daily basis. We are not comfortable with being uncomfortable; and, we consciously or subconsciously sidestep what we perceive to be vague, judgment-filled minefields. For this reason, more often than not, we are not in the spaces where authentic discussions about Confederate iconography and race relations are really happening. And, when we are in those spaces, we try to steer the conversation on the paths that feel safe for us—namely, back to seeing Confederate iconography discussions as artifact-based. Sadly, because of our standings in our communities, we can be seen in extremes—as experts (and, so, participants willingly follow us down these safe paths) or irrelevant bystanders (and, so, participants take anything that we say with a grain of salt at best and an eye roll at worst). If we want to be active participants in the *authentic* discussions that are happening, we need to step back and see more clearly where we fit as (personal and professional) individuals who have natural biases and motivations and as institution who are stewards of the past.

So, let's step back so that we can step forward more confidently. Where are these conversations being had and what precipitates them? Who are the people having authentic conversations and what *are* authentic conversations? And, what role should we be playing? People are having conversations across the United States every day, behind the closed doors of religious institutions, homes, and offices. For better or worse, people are using social media to express themselves. They are calling on likeminded friends, family, colleagues, and strangers to share in understanding and affirmation. What individuals so often are *not* doing is authentically communicating with people different from themselves. Herein lies the problem, the hurdle individuals must jump in order to have conversations that truly move the United States forward. When conflict arises, as it certainly does when we focus on the intersections of Confederate iconography and race relations, people tend to shy away from gathering with a wide spectrum of perspectives in one room together. And, even when people are in the same room, they will often not say to each other what they would have said to their family or friends behind closed doors. We live in a society where authentic—genuine—conversations rarely happen in a public forum. Conversations that do happen in public forums often have an immediate impact rather than a long-term impact; many times, public conversations happen during moments of racial strife or after a tragic event fueled by racism. These public forums satisfy a need to voice frustrations, give a reminder of a perceived racial hierarchy, or show that some action has been taken in order to calm tensions. And, for history organizations who live in the public space, instigating an authentic conversation within this context can seem dangerous. If organizations are slow to react, for whatever reason, the initial outrage of the event subsides and so does the imperative to have an authentic conversation. Organizations must know their own communities. For example, the Atlanta History Center has been progressive in calling on the community to engage in dialogue about the continuing problem of race relations in and around the city. There is, in some respects, more leeway to have discussions about race in this southern city. The Missouri History Museum organized community discussions about the shooting death of Michael Brown in Ferguson, Missouri, long after the international spotlight had shifted from the city. Through it all, the focus was not just on Michael Brown, but on the community—its genuine need for reconciliation and its continued issues with racial disparity, educational inequality, and housing segregation.

Where We Go From Here

Taking a critical look at the extent to which community conversations are (or are not) happening is not a judgment of organizations in our field; it is candidly laying the cards out on the table so that we can move forward in our discussion of what role we should actually be playing as we stand at the intersection of Confederate iconography, race relations, and public history. While on some level everyone is talking about ideas surrounding Confederate iconography (even if they are not using that particular phrase), we might narrow "people" down to groups of community stakeholders like city council members, religious leaders, educators, the chamber of commerce and the convention and visitors bureau, and a wide variety of heritage affinity groups. For example, the Blue Ribbon Commission on Race, Monuments and Public Spaces in Charlottesville, Virginia included representatives from the Human Rights Commission, PLACE Design Task Force, and the Historic Resources Committee.

Authentic conversations surrounding Confederate iconography can be held 1) if everyone who should be at the table is at the table so that all voices can be heard, 2) if there is a commitment to maintaining respect throughout the conversation, 3) if genuine listening occurs, and 4) if there is a sincere interest in making the best decision for all of the people involved. There are a number of ways to facilitate dialogues in order to support authentic conversations. The International Coalition of Sites of Conscience excels at facilitating dialogic arcs.[4] The Arc of Dialogue includes four phases: community-building, sharing the diversity of experiences about the topic at hand, exploring the diversity of experiences beyond each individual's personal experiences, and synthesizing and closing the learning experience.

Some organizations and some public historians are better trained for facilitating these conversations while others are better placed to hold the public space and bring in experienced facilitators. And, still other organizations will be best served by simply taking a seat in the dialogic circle and participating with genuine respect, active listening, and a willingness to come out of the learning experience with actions to make their organizations more inclusive and culturally responsive. Perhaps the most important lesson, and the hardest, that we will have to learn is that our communities do not need us to tell them what to do with the community's Confederate iconography. The display of monuments, memorials, flags, and even mascots and street names are products of both the community's past and its present. If we believe (or allow others to believe) that we are the experts and have the answers to what to do about Confederate monuments and memorials, then we are first doing our communities a disservice and second placing a new obstacle in the way of reconciliation and healing.

That is not to say that public historians and history organizations do not have expertise to offer during these discussions. First, being able to provide a physical space that is seen as neutral is important to the facilitation of authentic conversations. Second, public historians can provide valuable contexts to the discussion about the history of their community's historical Confederate iconography and race relations. In order to facilitate deeper and more authentic conversations, clearly acknowledging the complexities that surround the monuments and memorials themselves, historical stakeholders' motivations, and other historical contexts is important in dispelling potential assumptions and oversimplified understandings of the community's current affiliations with Confederate iconography. By making these efforts to lay a foundation for building greater empathy, we can hope to frame the conversation in a way that accepts (and to some extent embraces) the broad range of emotions that will be a major presence throughout the conversation. At the same time that there is an increase in clarity of content, there should be an equal increase in social/emotional validation.

While we act as professional stewards of history and do our best to preserve it, we must also acknowledge those things a community may need in order to heal. That may or may not include contextualizing monuments and images using new signage and panels or even developing signage that supports the history of why a particular monument has been replaced or is no longer visible. Without federal or state laws governing what is to be done across the board, it is the right of the community to decide whether or not they want to keep Confederate iconography visible or even transition that space into something totally different. It is important to empower individuals to come together to make the best decision for the community. And, part of that empowerment lies in more deeply understanding the place in which they live, work, and thrive. When many of these monuments and memorials were erected, the collective voice of the community was not heard or acknowledged. Monuments erected were often funded by donations raised by the United Daughters of the Confederacy. The United Daughters of the Confederacy often placed the location of Confederate monuments and memorials in prime locations within communities, often in the middle of town squares or other highly trafficked areas.[5] Without soliciting input from members of the community who did not wish to honor deceased Confederate soldiers (for whatever reason), these monuments have stood for decades never truly having the full support of the community. Some may argue an implicit acceptance, which is to some degree support; however, implicit acceptance through silence should never be an acceptable goal. In moving forward, it is essential that actively listening to voices that have previously been silenced (or unheard) will provide an opportunity for individuals and communities to more fully understand the impact of the past and how those interactions have influenced contemporary relationships, social/cultural structures, and racial legacies within communities.

We may intellectually acknowledge that the history symbolized by monuments and memorials would not be erased if the physical symbols were removed. However, it is sometimes more difficult to acknowledge our own personal and/or professional attachments. These attachments could be ties to personal heritage or even job security. Emotional connections aside, we intellectually know that the past is not automatically doomed to be repeated if there is not a visual reminder; and, lessons are not learned just because a physical reference can be glanced at from time to time as we pass by. Facing the past doesn't have to be literal; and, it might be more impactful if it were not.

As it stands, there is clear evidence that the Confederate flag has psychological power. An experiment that was published in the journal *Political Psychology* in 2011 reported how strongly the Confederate flag continues to prompt racist attitudes.[6] While stereotypes and research from years past center the tie between Confederate flags and racist attitudes on white southerners, photographs, social media, and news reports prior to and after the 2016 presidential election clearly show that the use of Confederate flags alongside racist attitudes is not confined to one demographic or geographic area. There has also been research that proposes that nationally recognized symbols are not passive, but actually yield significant psychological and social effects whether consciously or subconsciously. National symbols seem to enhance feelings of group unity and identification; and, empirical data concludes that national symbols have important implications for intergroup dynamics.[7] So, whether a person believes him- or herself to have a strong, weak, or non-reaction to Confederate iconography, there is a psychological effect taking place. Confederate iconography does influence a person's identity and the perception of where he/she belongs in society. This would additionally introduce an argument that the more consistently an individual is influenced by seeing Confederate iconography over a period of time, the deeper the residual effects would be. While many of us would like to believe that we live in a post-racial United States, that inclusion is a reality (not just an idea), and that we embrace being a "salad bowl" rather than a "melting pot," recent news suggests otherwise. We are not post anything, not even close.

Conclusion

We must contextualize both the past and the present as they relate *to each other* if we want to confront the racial history of the United States and how that history has shaped the present and will undoubtedly shape the future. Reconciliation is a process that takes time, patience, and trust. As individuals and organizations, we can assist with fostering these relationships by providing current scholarship that helps communities understand where they have been, where they are and help them set the stage to get to where they want to be. If communities decide to remove local Confederate iconography, public historians can offer best practices to ensure that these monuments are preserved within the collections of partnering cultural institutions that have the capacity, ability, and the desire to continue programs that delve into the deep complexities of their local iconographical artifacts. If communities decide to maintain monuments and memorials in their present locations, but want to rewrite the content of wayside markers in order to provide more context and complexity to the space then public historians should be there to support the research and writing of the new interpretation. In short, we need to be active participants not only in the dialogues, but in the collective next steps following the conversations. In acknowledging our strengths and weaknesses, as individuals and as a field, let us put down the weight of trying to be *the* leader of the process and instead, accept our roles as being *a part* of the process.

In retrospect, it is perfectly acceptable to be hesitant to jump into a discussion about what to do about Confederate memorials and monuments. It is not surprising that people feel strongly about whether Confederate flags should be removed. And, having the courage to speak authentically in public spaces about race relations often takes more bravery than discussing many other topics that reverberate within the walls of our institutions. However, here we stand at the crossroads once again—the intersections of Confederate iconography, race relations, and public history have been spotlighted for even the most oblivious to see. Now is the time to actively participate in the healing of our communities, our nation. In order to do that, we must first come to terms with our own emotions, biases, and motivations. We must internally admit that there are wrongs that need to be righted that we and our institutions have been a part of on some level. We must clarify for our staffs, volunteers, and stakeholders what we will stand for and what we will not tolerate as we work to usher in a new era of reconciliation; this era should be built on empathy, inclusion, and respect for all. Don't simply accept the most obvious answers or arguments; delve deeper and search for underlying motivations. Do the motivations of the past still have relevance today? Do our individual motivations hinder us from seeing another's point of view? Are we motivated by a desire to maintain our intellectual identities or our emotional identities? It's time to step back, take a deep breath, and reevaluate so that we can step forward more resolutely.

Notes

1. History Relevance Campaign, "The Value of History: Seven Ways It Is Essential," accessed December 4, 2016, http://historyrelevance.com/value-statement.
2. William Faulkner, *Requiem for a Nun* (New York: Random House, 1951).
3. Pierce Brown, *Morning Star* (New York: Random House, 2016).
4. Tammy Bormann, "Designing the Arc of Dialogue," International Coalition of Sites of Conscience, accessed December 4, 2016, http://sitesofconscience.org/wp-content/uploads/2012/10/Members_member-Benefits_010.pdf.
5. Karen Cox, *Dixie's Daughters: The United Daughters of the Confederacy and the Preservation of Confederate Culture* (University Press of Florida: Gainesville, 2003).
6. Joyce Ehrlinger, E. Ashby Plant, Richard P. Eibach, Corey J. Columb, Joanna L. Goplen, Jonathan W. Kunstman, and David A. Butz, "How Exposure to the Confederate Flag Affects Willingness to Vote for Barack Obama," *Political Psychology*, 32, no. 1 (February 2011): 131–46.
7. David Butz, "National Symbols as Agents of Psychological and Social Change," *Political Psychology*, 30, no. 5 (July 2009): 779–804.

Bibliography

Bailey, Louise N., Mary L. Morgan, and Carolyn R. Taylor, *Biographical Directory of the South Carolina Senate*. Columbia: University of South Carolina Press, 1986.

Blight, David W. *Race and Reunion: The Civil War in American Memory*. Cambridge: Harvard University Press, 2001.

Brundage, W. Fitzhugh. *The Southern Past: A Clash of Race and Memory*. Cambridge: Harvard University Press, 2005.

Cook, Robert J. *Troubled Commemoration: The American Civil War Centennial, 1961–1965*. Baton Rouge: Louisiana State University Press, 2007.

Coski, John M. *The Confederate Battle Flag: America's Most Embattled Emblem*. Cambridge: Harvard University Press, 2005.

Doss, Erika. *Memorial Mania: Public Feeling in America*. Chicago: Chicago University Press, 2010.

Eichstedt, Jennifer L., and Stephen Small. *Representations of Slavery: Race and Ideology in Southern Plantation Museums*. Washington, DC: Smithsonian Institution Press, 2002.

Gallas, Kristin L., and James DeWolf Perry, eds. *Interpreting Slavery at Museums and Historic Sites*. Lanham, MD: Rowman & Littlefield, 2015.

Goldfield, David. *Still Fighting the Civil War: The American South and Southern History*. Baton Rouge: Louisiana State University Press, 2002.

Horton, James Oliver, and Lois E. Horton, eds. *Slavery and Public History: The Tough Stuff of American Memory*. New York: New Press, 2006.

Janney, Caroline E. *Remembering the Civil War: Reunion and the Limits of Reconciliation*. Chapel Hill: University of North Carolina Press, 2013.

Levin, Kevin M. *Remembering the Battle of the Crater: War as Murder*. Lexington: University Press of Kentucky, 2012.

Levinson, Sanford. *Written in Stone: Public Monuments in Changing Societies*. Durham, NC: Duke University Press, 1998.

Linenthal, Edward T. *Sacred Ground: Americans and Their Battlefields*. Urbana: University of Illinois Press, 1991.

Rosenzweig, Roy, and David Thelen. *The Presence of the Past: Popular Uses of History in American Life*. New York: Columbia University Press, 1998.

Savage, Kirk. *Standing Soldiers, Kneeling Slaves: Race, War, and Monument in Nineteenth-Century America*. Princeton: Princeton University Press, 1997.

Shackel, Paul A., ed. *Myth, Memory, and the Making of the American Landscape*. Gainesville: University Press of Florida, 2001.

Sutton, Robert K., ed. *Rally on the High Ground: The National Park Service Symposium on the Civil War, Ford's Theatre, May 8 and 9, 2000*. Fort Washington, PA: Eastern National, 2001.

Index

Roof visit at, 73–74; survey of interpreters at, 62–63; trading card program at, 66–67. *See also individual parks*

National Portrait Gallery, 40

National Trust for Historic Preservation, 43

Native Americans, 29–30

Newman, I. DeQuincey, 81

OAH. *See* Organization of American Historians

Obama, Barack, 68, 83

O'Dell, Peggy, 63

Organization of American Historians (OAH), 62

Pamplin Historical Park, xv, 28

Parks, Rosa, xiv

Patterson, Kay, 81

Perot, H. Ross, 40

Petersburg National Battlefield, xv

Pinckney, Clementa C., 73, 83–84

Pond, James, 35

Powell, Robert, 46

public historians, outreach by, 95–99

Quarlls, Caroline, 35

Ralston, David, 51

Randolph, A. Philip, xiv

reconciliation and reunion, xiii

Reconstruction, xiv, xvi, 54, 88

Richmond, Virginia: Monument Avenue in, 3–4, 11–2; museums in, 9; tourism in, 8–9

Richmond National Battlefield Park, 6

Riley, Joe, 82

Robinson, James, 55

Richard Robison, 55

Robertson, Allen, 84

Romney, Mitt, 83

Roof, Dylann, xvi, 72, 83

Roosevelt, Franklin D. 41, 78

SCCWCC. *See* South Carolina Confederate Civil War Centennial Commission

SCCWSAB. *See* South Carolina Civil War Sesquicentennial Advisory Board

Scott, Tim, 83

SCV. *See* Sons of Confederate Veterans

Selma Interpretive Center, 68

Selma to Montgomery National Historical Trail, 68

Sheehan, Vincent, 83

Sherman, William Tecumseh, 53

Shiloh National Military Park, 67

Sinclair, Tim, 68, 70

slavery, xi, xiii, 1–2, 23, 29, 35, 45–46, 53, 68, 71; interpretation of, xiv–xix, 2, 5, 23, 47, 50, 52, 72, 85

Smith, Leroy, 84

Smith, Verne, 81

Sons of Confederate Veterans (SCV), 7, 78–79, 81, 85

South Carolina Confederate Civil War Centennial Commission (SCCWCC), 79, 81, 85

South Carolina Civil War Sesquicentennial Advisory Board (SCCWSAB), 86

South Carolina State Museum, 86

Special Field Order Number 15, 50

Stern, Marc J., 62

Stones River National Battlefield, 67

Stonewall Jackson House, xv

Strobel, Sylvia, 70

Taylor, Sandy, 68

Tenement Museum, 62

Thurmond, Michael, 49, 52, 54

Till, Emmett, xiv

Tosh, John, 62

UDC. *See* United Daughters of the Confederacy

Underground Railroad, 29

United Daughters of the Confederacy (UDC), 7, 19, 79, 97

United Confederate Veterans, 78

United States Colored Troops, 50, 67

About the Editor

Kevin M. Levin is an award-winning historian and educator based in Boston and has taught American history on both the high school and college levels. He has written and lectured widely on the Civil War era, historical memory, and public history. His first book, *Remembering the Battle of the Crater: War as Murder*, was published in 2012. His current book project, titled *Searching for Black Confederate Soldiers: The Civil War's Most Persistent Myth*, is under contract. His work has appeared online at *The Daily Beast*, *Smithsonian*, the *Atlantic*, and *The New York Times*. Over the years he has led numerous professional development workshops for history teachers at Ford's Theatre, the National Park Service, Massachusetts Historical Society, and Yale's Gilder-Lehrman Center. He currently serves on the board of directors of the National Council for History Education.

About the Contributors

Dina Bailey is CEO of Mountain Top Vision, a consulting company that focuses on supporting change management in the areas of diversity, inclusion, and strategic planning in order to increase audience engagement. She was previously director of Educational Strategies for the National Center for Civil and Human Rights and director of Museum Experiences for the National Underground Railroad Freedom Center. Dina holds a Bachelors in middle and secondary education, a Masters in anthropology of development and social transformation, and a graduate certification in museum studies. She has been published in both the formal education and museum fields. Dina is proud to be a board member of the American Association for State and Local History, the Association of African American Museums, the Next Generation Men, and the Issues Chair for the American Alliance of Museums' Education Committee.

Dr. Mark Benbow is assistant professor of history at Marymount University. He earned his PhD from Ohio University. From 1987 to 2002 he worked on national security issues for the federal government and from 2003 to 2006. Benbow was the historian at the Woodrow Wilson House Museum in Washington, DC. Since 2011 he has served as director of the Arlington Historical Museum in Arlington, Virginia. Benbow's first book, *Leading Them to the Promised Land: Woodrow Wilson, Covenant Theology and the Mexican Revolution: 1913–1915*, was published in 2010. His articles have appeared in *Journalism History*, *Studies in Intelligence*, *Journal of the Gilded Age and Progressive Era*, and *Brewery History* as well as essays in books on Wilson, on American foreign policy, and in specialized reference works. His biography of DC brewer Christian Heurich published in spring 2017.

Christy S. Coleman began her career as living history interpreter at the Colonial Williamsburg Foundation. Over the course of a ten-year career, she had increasing levels of responsibility finally serving as director of historic programs. In 1999 she was named president and CEO of the nation's largest African American museum, the Charles H. Wright Museum of African American History in Detroit, Michigan. In 2008, Coleman was named president and CEO of the American Civil War Center at Historic Tredegar. In 2013 she helped orchestrate the merger of the Center at Tredegar with the Museum of the Confederacy to create the American Civil War Museum serving as co-CEO. In May 2016 she was named CEO of the museum. Coleman has lectured extensively and consulted with some of the country's leading museums, written a number of scholarly and public history articles, as well as being an award-winning screenwriter for educational television.

Doug Dammann is education department coordinator at the Civil War Museum, part of the Kenosha Public Museum system in Kenosha, Wisconsin, where he oversees the development and presentation of all workshops, public programs, demonstrations, guided tours, and first person performances at the museum. Dammann also assists the Collections and Exhibits Department of the museum in the acquisition of museum artifacts and the development of exhibitions and audio/visual presentations. He is also a specialist in Civil War history and artifacts. Dammann came to the Civil War Museum after working in the collections and education departments of the National Air and Space Museum, Smithsonian Institution, and the National Museum of Civil War Medicine. He received his bachelor's degree in American history from Kalamazoo (MI) College and a master's in historical administration from Eastern Illinois University.

Jennifer Edginton is curator of education at the Kenosha Public Museums where she develops and implements school and public programming. She also develops and maintains the interpretive plan and evaluation protocol for the museums. Jennifer has over ten years of experience in museum education with past positions at the Museum of Science and Industry, The Field Museum, and Naper Settlement.

W. Eric Emerson is director of the South Carolina Department of Archives and History and State Historic Preservation Officer. During the 150th anniversary of the Civil War, he served as chair of the South Carolina Civil War Sesquicentennial Advisory Board and authored a number of articles regarding the commemoration. He serves on the AASLH Editorial Board and represents AASLH on the National Historic Publications and Records Commission. He also serves on the University of South Carolina Press Committee and on the finance committee for the Council of State Archivists. A native of Charlotte, North Carolina, he holds a BA in history from UNC-Charlotte and a MA and PhD in history from the University of Alabama. He began his career in public history as editor of the *South Carolina Historical Magazine* and later served as executive director of the South Carolina Historical Society and the Charleston Library Society. He has edited three annotated editions of Civil War letters and is the author of *Sons of Privilege: The Charleston Light Dragoons in the Civil War* (2006). He currently serves as vice chair of the South Carolina Hall of Fame and is the editor of *Palmetto Profiles: The South Carolina Encyclopedia Guide to the South Carolina Hall of Fame* (2013).

W. Todd Groce is president and CEO of the Georgia Historical Society. Born in Virginia and reared in Tennessee, Groce holds three degrees in history, including a PhD from the University of Tennessee, and a certificate in leadership development from the US Army War College. Before joining the Georgia Historical Society in 1995, Groce taught history at the University of Tennessee and Maryville College and was for five years executive director of the East Tennessee Historical Society. He is the author of *Mountain Rebels: East Tennessee Confederates and the Civil War* and co-editor with Stephen V. Ash of *Nineteenth-Century America: Essays in Honor of Paul H. Bergeron*. He has written more than fifty articles and book reviews for publications ranging from the *The Journal of Southern History* to *The New York Times* and he has made television appearances on the History Channel, Discovery

Channel, and CSPAN. A graduate of Leadership Georgia and past president of the Rotary Club of Savannah, he has been listed by *Georgia Trend* magazine as among the "100 Most Influential Georgians."

Dan Joyce has been director of the Kenosha Public Museums in Kenosha, Wisconsin (Kenosha Public Museum, Dinosaur Discovery Museum, and The Civil War Museum) since 2011. A graduate of Southern Illinois University and Eastern New Mexico University, he holds degrees in anthropology, American history, and museum studies. He has been a museum professional for forty years and archaeologist for over thirty years. During that time, he has held museum positions at Southern Illinois University Museum, The Field Museum, Blackwater Draw Archaeological Museum, Miles Anthropological Museum, the Kenosha Public Museum, The Civil War Museum, and the Dinosaur Discovery Museum. He is an IMLS, AAM MAP, and AAM Accreditation reviewer. He has published sixty articles on military history and archaeology, numerous archaeological reports, and is an elected fellow of the Company of Military Historians. He has presented twenty-nine papers and posters at professional conferences and is an adjunct professor in museology at the University of Wisconsin–Parkside. Before he became director, Dan was responsible for coordinating and overseeing all aspects of exhibit and collections work at the Kenosha Public Museums for twenty-five years. He designed and/or supervised more than two hundred temporary exhibits during that time. He was intimately involved in the design and functionality of the new Kenosha Public Museum, the Dinosaur Discovery Museum, and The Civil War Museum buildings and was responsible for all aspects of exhibit development and research.

Nicole A. Moore is a public historian who has worked in the museum field for more than seven years as an historic interpreter and museum educator. She holds degrees from the University of North Carolina at Charlotte in psychology (BA 2004) and history (MA 2008). As a museum professional, Nicole has presented at multiple conferences, including the National Council on Public History, the American Association of State and Local History, the Association of American Geographers, and the Slave Dwelling Conference. She has also held training sessions on interpreting slavery at Historic St. Mary's City in Maryland, Historic Brattonsville in McConnells, South Carolina, and Andrew Jackson's Hermitage, with a focus on how to address difficult histories and narratives with visitors. Nicole is proud to be part of the interpretive staff of Inalienable Rights, the living history component of the Slave Dwelling Project. A published author, Nicole has written about race and perception and its impact on how slavery is interpreted at historic sites. She is an active member of The National Council on Public History, the American Association for State and Local History, and the Southern Historical Association and serves on committees in all three organizations.

James A. Percoco is a nationally recognized history educator, with thirty-three years of teaching experience grades 6–12, and the recipient of numerous educational awards. He is the author of four books including *Summers with Lincoln: Looking for the Man in the Monuments* and *A Passion for the Past Creative Teaching of US History* as well as the forthcoming book, *Take the Journey: Teaching American History Through Place-Based Learning*. In 2011 he was inducted into the National Teachers Hall of Fame.

John Matthew Rudy works as a park ranger and interpretive trainer with the National Park Service's Interpretive Development Program in Harpers Ferry, West Virginia, creating interpretive training materials for park rangers and interpreters across the entire park system. Breaking new ground in audience-centered experiences and facilitating dialogue for the National Park Service, the Interpretive Development Program has been a leader in pushing the National Park Service to use new and innovative communication strategies to help visitors find deep meaning in park resources. His area of interest includes the history of abolition, the coming of the Civil War, the impact of war on everyday Americans, and the racial dynamics in the aftermath of emancipation. Rudy holds a master of arts in applied history from Shippensburg University and a bachelor of arts in history, with a minor in Civil War–era studies from Gettysburg College. He also teaches undergraduate courses as an adjunct instructor in the Civil War Era Studies Department at Gettysburg College.